LEARNING FROM LAS VEGAS

LEARNING FROM LAS VEGAS: THE FORGOTTEN SYMBOLISM OF ARCHITECTURAL FORM

Robert Venturi
Denise Scott Brown
Steven Izenour

The MIT Press
Cambridge, Massachusetts, and London, England

Originally published as *Learning from Las Vegas*

This book was set in IBM Composer Baskerville by Techdata Associates, printed on R&E Book by Murray Printing Company, and bound by Murray Printing Company in the United States of America.

Second printing, 1978
Third printing, 1978

Library of Congress Cataloging in Publication Data

Venturi, Robert.
    Learning from Las Vegas.

    Bibliography: p.
    1. Architecture—Nevada—Las Vegas. 2. Symbolism in architecture. I. Scott Brown, Denise, 1931-   , joint author. II. Izenour, Steven, joint author. III. Title.
NA735.L3V4   1977   720'.9793'13   77-1917
ISBN 0-262-22020-2 (hardcover)
ISBN 0-262-72006-X (paperback)

TO ROBERT SCOTT BROWN, 1931-1959

CONTENTS

PREFACE TO THE FIRST EDITION

The first part of this book is a description of our study of the architecture of the commercial strip. Part II is a generalization on symbolism in architecture and the iconography of urban sprawl from our findings in Part I.

"Passing through Las Vegas is Route 91, the archetype of the commercial strip, the phenomenon at its purest and most intense. We believe a careful documentation and analysis of its physical form is as important to architects and urbanists today as were the studies of medieval Europe and ancient Rome and Greece to earlier generations. Such a study will help to define a new type of urban form emerging in America and Europe, radically different from that we have known; one that we have been ill-equipped to deal with and that, from ignorance, we define today as urban sprawl. An aim of this studio will be, through open-minded and nonjudgmental investigation, to come to understand this new form and to begin to evolve techniques for its handling."

So started the introduction to a studio we conducted at the Yale School of Art and Architecture in the fall of 1968. It was, in fact, a research project, undertaken as a collaboration among three instructors, nine students of architecture, and two planning and two graphics students in graduate programs at Yale. The studio was entitled "Learning from Las Vegas, or Form Analysis as Design Research." Toward the end of the semester, as the spirit of Las Vegas got to them, the students changed the second name to "The Great Proletarian Cultural Locomotive."

We spent three weeks in the library, four days in Los Angeles, and ten days in Las Vegas. We returned to Yale and spent ten weeks analyzing and presenting our discoveries. Before this, we authors had visited Las Vegas several times and written "A Significance for A&P Parking Lots, or Learning from Las Vegas" (*Architectural Forum*, March 1968); this formed the basis for the research program that we drafted during the summer of 1968. We divided the work into twelve topics, to be assigned to individuals or small groups, and into five phases, including Phase III, "Applied Research," in Las Vegas. The first part of this book contains our original article augmented by the findings of the research project. Unfortunately, with twelve or so people, we were not able to cover all the research topics we had programmed, nor did we have available time or data to cover other subjects adequately. There is still a wealth of architectural information to be culled from Las Vegas. In addition, some of the emphases that were important to the studio we have not stressed in this book; for example, our pedagogical interest in evolving the traditional architectural "studio" into a new tool for teaching architecture and our particular interest in finding graphic means, more suitable than those now used by architects and planners, to describe "urban sprawl" urbanism and particularly the commercial strip.

Las Vegas met our project with courtesy and helpfulness at the technical, planning agency level and with courtesy and unhelpfulness at the decision making level. No funds were available at city or county hall, and the chairman of the Strip Beautification Committee felt that Yale should pay Las Vegas to make the study. The day of our arrival a local paper announced, "Yale Professor Will Praise Strip for $8,925." A few days later when, still hopeful, we requested a further sum for the making of a film, the newspaper rebounded, "Yale Professor Ups Price to Praise Strip." The nearest we came to official financial support was a reduction in the hourly price on the use of Mr. Howard Hughes's helicopter.

Our ideas too were met with polite skepticism, and we gathered that the Beautification Committee would continue to recommend turning the Strip into a western Champs Elysées, obscuring the signs with trees and raising the humidity level with giant fountains, and that the local planning and zoning agencies would continue to try to persuade the gasoline stations to imitate the architecture of the casinos, in the interest of architectural unity.

On the other hand, the Stardust Hotel, one of the finest on the Strip, gave us all free board and lodging. The car rental agencies combined to give us a week's free use of a car. And the Young Electric Sign Company (YESCO), in particular Mr. Vaughan Cannon, constituted itself our chief host and helper in Las Vegas. In addition, we are grateful to Mr. Jerry Litman, then of the *Las Vegas Sun*, for trying to give our study a more friendly press. And finally, to the much-respected Las Vegas citizen who took one female Yale professor to the gala opening of the Circus Circus Casino, legally, and wangled, semilegally, an entry to this social highlight for the whole class—attired to meet the situation in Day-Glo-decorated castoffs from the local Salvation Army Store.

The temptation is great to augment the list of thank-yous to include all those to whom three people feel warmly grateful for help in their intellectual lives. The following list has been culled from that much larger list to include those who have been the particular intellectual and artistic underpinnings of this project. They are the late Donald Drew Egbert, Herbert J. Gans, J. B. Jackson, Louis Kahn, Arthur Korn, Jean Labatut, Esther McCoy, Robert B. Mitchell, Charles Moore, Lewis Mumford, the Pop artists (particularly Edward Ruscha), Vincent Scully, Charles Seeger, Melvin M. Webber, and Tom Wolfe. With some temerity we acknowledge too the help of Michelangelo, the Italian and English Mannerists, Sir Edwin Lutyens, Sir Patrick Geddes, Frank Lloyd Wright, and the early generations of Heroic Modern architects.

Because we have criticized Modern architecture, it is proper here to state our intense admiration of its early period when its founders, sensitive to their own times, proclaimed the right revolution. Our argument lies mainly with the irrelevant and distorted prolongation of that old revolution today. Similarly we have no argument with the many architects today who, having discovered in practice through economic pressure that the rhetoric of architectural revolution would not work, have jettisoned it and are building straightforward buildings in line with the needs of the client and the times. Nor is this a criticism of those architects and academics who are developing new approaches to architecture through research in allied fields and in scientific methods. These too are in part a reaction to the same architecture we have criticized. We think the more directions that architecture takes at this point, the better. Ours does not exclude theirs and vice versa.

Our more formal but heartfelt thanks for help with the studio go to Avis Car Rental, Las Vegas; The Celeste and Armand Bartos Foundation; Dennis Durden; the Honorable Oran Gragson, Mayor of Las Vegas; Dr. David Henry, Clark County Administrator; Hertz Car Rental, Las Vegas; George Izenour; Philip Johnson; The Edgar J. Kaufmann Foundation; Alan Lapidus; Morris Lapidus; National Car Rental, Las Vegas; The Ossabaw Island Project; The Nathaniel and Marjorie Owings Foundation; The Rohm and Haas Company, Philadelphia; the staff, Clark Country Planning Commission; the staff, Las Vegas City Planning Commission; U.C.L.A. School of Architecture and Urban Planning; Yale Reports; The Young Electric Sign Company, Las Vegas; and to all the people in and around the Yale School of Art and Architecture who pitched in and helped, especially Gert Wood; and to Dean Howard Weaver, Charles Moore, and Yale University, none of whom found it odd that Yale architects could have serious purposes in Las Vegas, and who picked up the tab when our meager sources of funding had been exhausted.

Our thanks also go to the students whose skill, energy, and wit fueled the great cultural locomotive and gave it its special character and who taught us how to live it up and learn in Las Vegas.

For the writing of the book, we thank the Edgar J. Kaufmann Foundation and the Celeste and Armand Bartos Foundation, both of which helped us a second time; the National Endowment for the Arts in Washington, D.C., a federal agency created by an Act of Congress, 1965; our firm, Venturi and Rauch, especially our partner, our Rauch of Gibraltar, for his sometimes grudging but always crucial support and for the sacrifices a small office makes when three of its members write a book; we thank Virginia Gordan and Dan and Carol Scully for their help and advice with the illustrations; and Janet Schueren and Carol

Rauch for typing the manuscript. And finally Steven Izenour, who is our co-worker, co-author, and *sine qua non.*

Denise Scott Brown and Robert Venturi   Calivigny Island, W. I.

PREFACE TO THE REVISED EDITION

This new edition of *Learning from Las Vegas* arose from the displeasure expressed by students and others at the price of the original version. Knowing that a second printing of the original version would be almost twice the original price, we have chosen instead to abridge the book to bring its ideas within the reach of those who would like to read it. At the same time, we have taken the opportunity to focus our argument more clearly and to add a little, so the new edition, although abridged, stands on its own and goes beyond its progenitor.

The main omissions are the final section, on our work, and about one-third of the illustrations, including almost all in color and those in black and white that could not be reduced to fit a smaller page size. Changes in format further reduce costs, but we hope that they will serve too, to shift the book's emphasis from illustrations to text, and to remove the conflict between our critique of Bauhaus design and the latter-day Bauhaus design of the book; the "interesting" Modern styling of the first edition, we felt, belied our subject matter, and the triple spacing of the lines made the text hard to read.

Stripped and newly clothed, the analyses of Part I and the theories of Part II should appear more clearly what we intended them to be: a treatise on symbolism in architecture. Las Vegas is not the subject of our book. The symbolism of architectural form is. Most alterations to the text (aside from corrections of errors and changes to suit the new format) are made to point up this focus. For the same reason we have added a subtitle, *The Forgotten Symbolism of Architectural Form*. A few more changes were made, elegantly, we hope, to "de-sex" the text. Following the saner, more humane custom of today, the architect is no longer referred to as "he."

This is not a suitable place to respond to our critics, but, as we intend to augment as well as to abridge, I shall list our replies made in other places.

Allegations that in studying Las Vegas we lacked social responsibility and concern are answered in an article entitled "On Architectural Formalism and Social Concern; a Discourse for Social Planners and Radical Chic Architects."

Since *Learning from Las Vegas* was written, the lights of Las Vegas have gone out for a spell and Americans' confidence in the automobile and other resources has been rocked in the first of possibly many crises. High energy expenditure and urban wastefulness are not central to our arguments for symbolic architecture and receptivity to other peoples' values; I tried to show why in an interview in *On Site on Energy*.

Robert Venturi's note on attribution in the first edition, with its request for fairness to his co-authors and co-workers, was virtually ignored by almost all reviewers. Personal pique at the cavalier handling of my contribution and at attributions in general by architects and journalists led me to analyze the social structure of the profession, its domination by upper-class males, and the emphasis its members place upon the architectural star system. The result is an article entitled "Sexism and the Star System in Architecture."

Source information on these and other articles may be found in the Venturi and Rauch bibliography which has been added to this edition. This list of writings by members of the firm and others is the most complete we have. We welcome information on anything we have omitted.

Since the publication of this book our thoughts on symbolism in architecture have been developed through several different projects. The Yale architecture studio that gave rise to *Learning from Las Vegas* was followed the next year by a study of architectural symbolism in residential suburbia, entitled "Remedial Housing for Architects, or Learning from Levittown." This material forms part of "Signs of Life: Symbols in the American City," a Bicentennial exhibition we designed for the National Collection of Fine Arts of the Smithsonian Institution at the Renwick Gallery. In similar vein, an article, "Symbols, Signs and Aesthetics: Architectural Taste in a Pluralist Society," comments on the social content of architectural symbolism and on the relation of architects to the different taste cultures of our society; and another, "Architecture as Shelter with Decoration on It," amplifies our theories on symbolism.

Questions of architectural pedagogy were of great concern in the two Yale projects but were merely hinted at in *Learning from Las Vegas*. In this revised version the parallel text of studio notes has been removed to a separate section and keyed to the Part I text. In this form it reestablishes something of its original identity. Further thoughts on architectural pedagogy, research, and studio are expounded in an article entitled "On Formal Analysis as Design Research, with Some Notes on Studio Pedagogy."

Publications on our architectural work are listed in the bibliography. Fairly recent broad-scale coverage has been given our firm in two issues of Japanese *Architecture and Urbanism*.

In the nine years since our study was initiated, Las Vegas and the Strip have changed too. Some buildings have new wings and restyled facades. Some signs are no longer there. Delicate and intense neon high readers have given way to bland, white, plastic, rear-illuminated message boards that alter the scale and vitality of Strip ornament. Portes cocheres now vie with signs as bearers of symbolic information.

We sense that the ideas initiated in *Learning from Las Vegas* are receiving much greater acceptance than when they were first published. We feel too that architects, bar a few diehards, are coming to realize that what we learned from Las Vegas, and what they by implication should learn too, is not to place neon signs on the Champs Elysées or a blinking "2 + 2 = 4" on the roof of the Mathematics Building, but rather to reassess the role of symbolism in architecture, and, in the process, to learn a new receptivity to the tastes and values of other people and a new modesty in our designs and in our perception of our role as architects in society. Architecture for the last quarter of our century should be socially less coercive and aesthetically more vital than the striving and bombastic buildings of our recent past. We architects can learn this from Rome and Las Vegas and from looking around us wherever we happen to be.

Denise Scott Brown   West Mount Airy, Philadelphia

PART I

A SIGNIFICANCE FOR
A&P PARKING LOTS,
OR LEARNING FROM LAS VEGAS

§ A SIGNIFICANCE FOR A&P PARKING LOTS, OR LEARNING FROM LAS VEGAS

"Substance for a writer consists not merely of those realities he thinks he discovers; it consists even more of those realities which have been made available to him by the literature and idioms of his own day and by the images that still have vitality in the literature of the past. Stylistically, a writer can express his feeling about this substance either by imitation, if it sits well with him, or by parody, if it doesn't."[1]

Learning from the existing landscape is a way of being revolutionary for an architect. Not the obvious way, which is to tear down Paris and begin again, as Le Corbusier suggested in the 1920s, but another, more tolerant way; that is, to question how we look at things.

The commercial strip, the Las Vegas Strip in particular—the example par excellence (Figs. 1 and 2)—challenges the architect to take a positive, non-chip-on-the-shoulder view. Architects are out of the habit of looking nonjudgmentally at the environment, because orthodox Modern architecture is progressive, if not revolutionary, utopian, and puristic; it is dissatisfied with *existing* conditions. Modern architecture has been anything but permissive: Architects have preferred to change the existing environment rather than enhance what is there.

But to gain insight from the commonplace is nothing new: Fine art often follows folk art. Romantic architects of the eighteenth century discovered an existing and conventional rustic architecture. Early Modern architects appropriated an existing and conventional industrial vocabulary without much adaptation. Le Corbusier loved grain elevators and steamships; the Bauhaus looked like a factory; Mies refined the details of American steel factories for concrete buildings. Modern architects work through analogy, symbol, and image—although they have gone to lengths to disclaim almost all determinants of their forms except structural necessity and the program—and they derive insights, analogies, and stimulation from unexpected images. There is a perversity in the learning process: We look backward at history and tradition to go forward; we can also look downward to go upward. And withholding judgment may be used as a tool to make later judgment more sensitive. This is a way of learning from everything.

§ COMMERCIAL VALUES AND COMMERCIAL METHODS

Las Vegas is analyzed here only as a phenomenon of architectural

§ See material under the corresponding heading in the Studio Notes section following Part I.

1. Richard Poirier, "T. S. Eliot and the Literature of Waste," *The New Republic* (May 20, 1967), p. 21.

4

1. The Las Vegas Strip, looking southwest

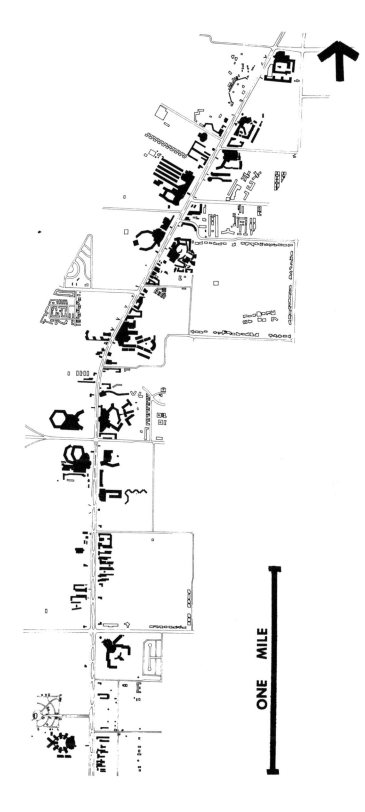

ONE MILE

2. Map of Las Vegas Strip

communication. Just as an analysis of the structure of a Gothic cathedral need not include a debate on the morality of medieval religion, so Las Vegas's values are not questioned here. The morality of commercial advertising, gambling interests, and the competitive instinct is not at issue here, although, indeed, we believe it should be in the architect's broader, *synthetic* tasks of which an analysis such as this is but one aspect. The analysis of a drive-in church in this context would match that of a drive-in restaurant, because this is a study of method, not content. Analysis of one of the architectural variables in isolation from the others is a respectable scientific and humanistic activity, so long as all are resynthesized in design. Analysis of existing American urbanism is a socially desirable activity to the extent that it teaches us architects to be more understanding and less authoritarian in the plans we make for both inner-city renewal and new development. In addition, there is no reason why the methods of commercial persuasion and the skyline of signs analyzed here should not serve the purpose of civic and cultural enhancement. But this is not entirely up to the architect.

BILLBOARDS ARE ALMOST ALL RIGHT

Architects who can accept the lessons of primitive vernacular architecture, so easy to take in an exhibit like "Architecture without Architects," and of industrial, vernacular architecture, so easy to adapt to an electronic and space vernacular as elaborate neo-Brutalist or neo-Constructivist megastructures, do not easily acknowledge the validity of the commercial vernacular. For the artist, creating the new may mean choosing the old or the existing. Pop artists have relearned this. Our acknowledgment of existing, commercial architecture at the scale of the highway is within this tradition.

Modern architecture has not so much excluded the commercial vernacular as it has tried to take it over by inventing and enforcing a vernacular of its own, improved and universal. It has rejected the combination of fine art and crude art. The Italian landscape has always harmonized the vulgar and the Vitruvian: the *contorni* around the *duomo*, the *portiere's* laundry across the *padrone's portone, Supercortemaggiore* against the Romanesque apse. Naked children have never played in *our* fountains, and I. M. Pei will never be happy on Route 66.

ARCHITECTURE AS SPACE

Architects have been bewitched by a single element of the Italian landscape: the piazza. Its traditional, pedestrian-scaled, and intricately enclosed space is easier to like than the spatial sprawl of Route 66 and

Los Angeles. Architects have been brought up on Space, and enclosed space is the easiest to handle. During the last 40 years, theorists of Modern architecture (Wright and Le Corbusier sometimes excepted) have focused on space as the essential ingredient that separates architecture from painting, sculpture, and literature. Their definitions glory in the uniqueness of the medium; although sculpture and painting may sometimes be allowed spatial characteristics, sculptural or pictorial architecture is unacceptable—because Space is sacred.

Purist architecture was partly a reaction against nineteenth-century eclecticism. Gothic churches, Renaissance banks, and Jacobean manors were frankly picturesque. The mixing of styles meant the mixing of media. Dressed in historical styles, buildings evoked explicit associations and romantic allusions to the past to convey literary, ecclesiastical, national, or programmatic symbolism. Definitions of architecture as space and form at the service of program and structure were not enough. The overlapping of disciplines may have diluted the architecture, but it enriched the meaning.

Modern architects abandoned a tradition of iconology in which painting, sculpture, and graphics were combined with architecture. The delicate hieroglyphics on a bold pylon, the archetypal inscriptions of a Roman architrave, the mosaic processions in Sant'Apollinare, the ubiquitous tattoos over a Giotto Chapel, the enshrined hierarchies around a Gothic portal, even the illusionistic frescoes in a Venetian villa, all contain messages beyond their ornamental contribution to architectural space. The integration of the arts in Modern architecture has always been called a good thing. But one did not paint *on* Mies. Painted panels were floated independently of the structure by means of shadow joints; sculpture was in or near but seldom on the building. Objects of art were used to reinforce architectural space at the expense of their own content. The Kolbe in the Barcelona Pavilion was a foil to the directed spaces: The message was mainly architectural. The diminutive signs in most Modern buildings contained only the most necessary messages, like LADIES, minor accents begrudgingly applied.

ARCHITECTURE AS SYMBOL

Critics and historians, who documented the "decline of popular symbols" in art, supported orthodox Modern architects, who shunned symbolism of form as an expression or reinforcement of content: meaning was to be communicated, not through allusion to previously known forms, but through the inherent, physiognomic characteristics of form. The creation of architectural form was to be a logical process, free from images of past experience, determined solely by program and structure, with an occasional assist, as Alan Colquhoun has suggested,[2] from intuition.

But some recent critics have questioned the possible level of content to be derived from abstract forms. Others have demonstrated that the functionalists, despite their protestations, derived a formal vocabulary of their own, mainly from current art movements and the industrial vernacular; and latter-day followers such as the Archigram group have turned, while similarly protesting, to Pop Art and the space industry. However, most critics have slighted a continuing iconology in popular commercial art, the persuasive heraldry that pervades our environment from the advertising pages of *The New Yorker* to the superbillboards of Houston. And their theory of the "debasement" of symbolic architecture in nineteenth-century eclecticism has blinded them to the value of the representational architecture along highways. Those who acknowledge this roadside eclecticism denigrate it, because it flaunts the cliché of a decade ago as well as the style of a century ago. But why not? Time travels fast today.

The Miami Beach Modern motel on a bleak stretch of highway in southern Delaware reminds jaded drivers of the welcome luxury of a tropical resort, persuading them, perhaps, to forgo the gracious plantation across the Virginia border called Motel Monticello. The real hotel in Miami alludes to the international stylishness of a Brazilian resort, which, in turn, derives from the International Style of middle Corbu. This evolution from the high source through the middle source to the low source took only 30 years. Today, the middle source, the neo-Eclectic architecture of the 1940s and the 1950s, is less interesting than its commercial adaptations. Roadside copies of Ed Stone are more interesting than the real Ed Stone.

§ SYMBOL IN SPACE BEFORE FORM IN SPACE: LAS VEGAS AS A COMMUNICATION SYSTEM

The sign for the Motel Monticello, a silhouette of an enormous Chippendale highboy, is visible on the highway before the motel itself. This architecture of styles and signs is antispatial; it is an architecture of communication over space; communication dominates space as an element in the architecture and in the landscape (Figs. 1-6). But it is for a new scale of landscape. The philosophical associations of the old eclecticism evoked subtle and complex meanings to be savored in the docile spaces of a traditional landscape. The commercial persuasion of roadside eclecticism provokes bold impact in the vast and complex setting of a new landscape of big spaces, high speeds, and complex programs.

2. Alan Colquhoun, "Typology and Design Method," *Arena,* Journal of the Architectural Association (June 1967), pp. 11-14.

Styles and signs make connections among many elements, far apart and seen fast. The message is basely commercial; the context is basically new.

A driver 30 years ago could maintain a sense of orientation in space. At the simple crossroad a little sign with an arrow confirmed what was obvious. One knew where one was. When the crossroads becomes a cloverleaf, one must turn right to turn left, a contradiction poignantly evoked in the print by Allan D'Arcangelo (Fig. 7). But the driver has no time to ponder paradoxical subtleties within a dangerous, sinuous maze. He or she relies on signs for guidance—enormous signs in vast spaces at high speeds.

The dominance of signs over space at a pedestrian scale occurs in big airports. Circulation in a big railroad station required little more than a simple axial system from taxi to train, by ticket window, stores, waiting room, and platform—all virtually without signs. Architects object to signs in buildings: "If the plan is clear, you can see where to go." But complex programs and settings require complex combinations of media beyond the purer architectural triad of structure, form, and light at the service of space. They suggest an architecture of bold communication rather than one of subtle expression.

§ THE ARCHITECTURE OF PERSUASION

The cloverleaf and airport communicate with moving crowds in cars or on foot for efficiency and safety. But words and symbols may be used in space for commercial persuasion (Figs. 6, 28). The Middle Eastern bazaar contains no signs; the Strip is virtually all signs (Fig. 8). In the bazaar, communication works through proximity. Along its narrow aisles, buyers feel and smell the merchandise, and the merchant applies explicit oral persuasion. In the narrow streets of the medieval town, although signs occur, persuasion is mainly through the sight and smell of the real cakes through the doors and windows of the bakery. On Main Street, shop-window displays for pedestrians along the sidewalks and exterior signs, perpendicular to the street for motorists, dominate the scene almost equally.

On the commercial strip the supermarket windows contain no merchandise. There may be signs announcing the day's bargains, but they are to be read by pedestrians approaching from the parking lot. The building itself is set back from the highway and half hidden, as is most of the urban environment, by parked cars (Fig. 9). The vast parking lot is in front, not at the rear, since it is a symbol as well as a convenience. The building is low because air conditioning demands low spaces, and merchandising techniques discourage second floors; its architecture is neutral because it can hardly be seen from the road. Both merchandise

3. Dunes Casino and Hotel, Las Vegas

4. Wedding chapel, Las Vegas

5. Stardust Casino and Hotel, Las Vegas

6. Night messages, Las Vegas

7. Allan D'Arcangelo, *The Trip*

DIRECTIONAL SPACE

	SPACE · SCALE	SPEED	SYMBOL sign-symbol·bldg ratio
EASTERN BAZAAR		3 M.P.H.	
MEDIEVAL STREET		3 M.P.H.	
MAIN STREET		3 M.P.H. 20 M.P.H.	
COMMERCIAL STRIP		35 M.P.H.	
THE STRIP		35 M.P.H.	
SHOPPING CENTER		3 M.P.H. 50 M.P.H.	

8. A comparative analysis of directional spaces

9. Parking lot of a suburban supermarket

10. Tanya billboard on the Strip

11. Lower Strip, looking north

and architecture are disconnected from the road. The big sign leaps to connect the driver to the store, and down the road the cake mixes and detergents are advertised by their national manufacturers on enormous billboards inflected toward the highway. The graphic sign in space has become the architecture of this landscape (Figs. 10, 11). Inside, the A&P has reverted to the bazaar except that graphic packaging has replaced the oral persuasion of the merchant. At another scale, the shopping center off the highway returns in its pedestrian malls to the medieval street.

§ VAST SPACE IN THE HISTORICAL TRADITION AND AT THE A&P

The A&P parking lot is a current phase in the evolution of vast space since Versailles (Fig. 12). The space that divides high-speed highway and low, sparse buildings produces no enclosure and little direction. To move through a piazza is to move between high enclosing forms. To move through this landscape is to move over vast expansive texture: the megatexture of the commercial landscape. The parking lot is the *parterre* of the asphalt landscape (Fig. 13). The patterns of parking lines give direction much as the paving patterns, curbs, borders, and *tapis vert* give direction in Versailles; grids of lamp posts substitute for obelisks, rows of urns and statues as points of identity and continuity in the vast space. But it is the highway signs, through their sculptural forms or pictorial silhouettes, their particular positions in space, their inflected shapes, and their graphic meanings, that identify and unify the megatexture. They make verbal and symbolic connections through space, communicating a complexity of meanings through hundreds of associations in few seconds from far away. Symbol dominates space. Architecture is not enough. Because the spatial relationships are made by symbols more than by forms, architecture in this landscape becomes symbol in space rather than form in space. Architecture defines very little: The big sign and the little building is the rule of Route 66.

The sign is more important than the architecture. This is reflected in the proprietor's budget. The sign at the front is a vulgar extravaganza, the building at the back, a modest necessity. The architecture is what is cheap. Sometimes the building is the sign: The duck store in the shape of a duck, called "The Long Island Duckling," (Figs. 14, 15) is sculptural symbol and architectural shelter. Contradiction between outside and inside was common in architecture before the Modern movement, particularly in urban and monumental architecture (Fig. 16). Baroque domes were symbols as well as spatial constructions, and they are bigger in scale and higher outside than inside in order to dominate their urban setting and communicate their symbolic message. The false fronts of

VAST SPACE

SPACE·SCALE

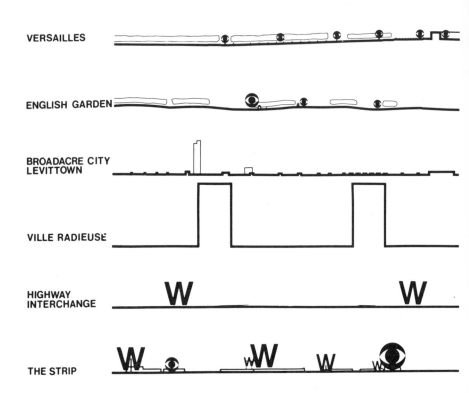

VERSAILLES

ENGLISH GARDEN

BROADACRE CITY
LEVITTOWN

VILLE RADIEUSE

HIGHWAY
INTERCHANGE

THE STRIP

SPACE · SCALE · SPEED · SYMBOL

12. A comparative analysis of vast spaces

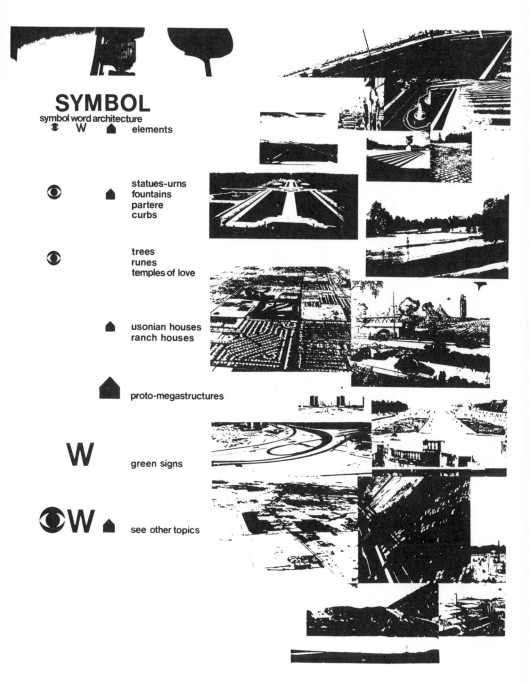

SYMBOL

symbol word architecture

● W ▲ elements

●   ▲ statues-urns
        fountains
        partere
        curbs

●   trees
        runes
        temples of love

      ▲ usonian houses
        ranch houses

      ▲ proto-megastructures

W   green signs

●W ▲ see other topics

13. Aladdin Casino and Hotel, Las Vegas

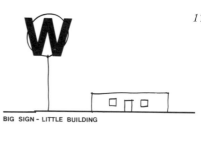

BIG SIGN - LITTLE BUILDING

OR

BUILDING IS SIGN

15. Big sign-little building or building as sign

14. "The Long Island Duckling" from *God's Own Junkyard*

SCALE SPEED SYMBOL

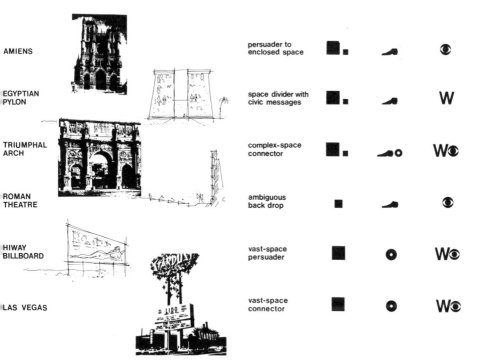

16. A comparative analysis of "billboards" in space

Western stores did the same thing: They were bigger and taller than the interiors they fronted to communicate the store's importance and to enhance the quality and unity of the street. But false fronts are of the order and scale of Main Street. From the desert town on the highway in the West of today, we can learn new and vivid lessons about an impure architecture of communication. The little low buildings, gray-brown like the desert, separate and recede from the street that is now the highway, their false fronts disengaged and turned perpendicular to the highway as big, high signs. If you take the signs away, there is no place. The desert town is intensified communication along the highway.

FROM ROME TO LAS VEGAS

Las Vegas is the apotheosis of the desert town. Visiting Las Vegas in the mid-1960s was like visiting Rome in the late 1940s. For young Americans in the 1940s, familiar only with the auto-scaled, gridiron city and the antiurban theories of the previous architectural generation, the traditional urban spaces, the pedestrian scale, and the mixtures, yet continuities, of styles of the Italian piazzas were a significant revelation. They rediscovered the piazza. Two decades later architects are perhaps ready for similar lessons about large open space, big scale, and high speed. Las Vegas is to the Strip what Rome is to the Piazza.

There are other parallels between Rome and Las Vegas: their expansive settings in the Campagna and in the Mojave Desert, for instance, that tend to focus and clarify their images. On the other hand, Las Vegas *was* built in a day, or rather, the Strip was developed in a virgin desert in a short time. It was not superimposed on an older pattern as were the pilgrim's Rome of the Counter-Reformation and the commercial strips of eastern cities, and it is therefore easier to study. Each city is an archetype rather than a prototype, an exaggerated example from which to derive lessons for the typical. Each city vividly superimposes elements of a supranational scale on the local fabric: churches in the religious capital, casinos and their signs in the entertainment capital. These cause violent juxtapositions of use and scale in both cities. Rome's churches, off streets and piazzas, are open to the public; the pilgrim, religious or architectural, can walk from church to church. The gambler or architect in Las Vegas can similarly take in a variety of casinos along the Strip. The casinos and lobbies of Las Vegas are ornamental and monumental and open to the promenading public; a few old banks and railroad stations excepted, they are unique in American cities. Nolli's map of the mid-eighteenth century reveals the sensitive and complex connections between public and private space in Rome (Fig. 17). Private building is shown in gray crosshatching that is carved into by the public spaces, exterior *and* interior. These spaces, open or roofed, are shown in minute detail through darker poché. Interiors of churches read like piazzas and courtyards of palaces, yet a variety of qualities and scales is articulated.

§   MAPS OF LAS VEGAS

A "Nolli" map of the Las Vegas Strip reveals and clarifies what is public and what is private, but here the scale is enlarged by the inclusion of the parking lot, and the solid-to-void ratio is reversed by the open spaces of the desert. Mapping the Nolli components from an aerial photograph provides an intriguing crosscut of Strip systems (Fig. 18). These components, separated and redefined, could be undeveloped land, asphalt, autos, buildings, and ceremonial space (Figs. 19 *a-e*). Reassembled, they describe the Las Vegas equivalent of the pilgrims' way, although the description, like Nolli's map, misses the iconological dimensions of the experience (Fig. 20).

A conventional land-use map of Las Vegas can show the overall structure of commercial use in the city as it relates to other uses but none of the detail of use type or intensity. "Land-use" maps of the insides of casino complexes, however, begin to suggest the systematic planning that all casinos share (Fig. 21). Strip "address" and "establishment" maps can depict both intensity and variety of use (Fig. 22). Distribution maps show patterns of, for example, churches, and food stores (Figs. 24, 25) that Las Vegas shares with other cities and those such as wedding chapels and auto rental stations (Figs. 26, 27) that are Strip-oriented and unique. It is extremely hard to suggest the atmospheric qualities of Las Vegas, because these are primarily dependent on watts (Fig. 23), animation, and iconology; however, "message maps," tourist maps, and brochures suggest some of it (Figs. 28, 71).

§   MAIN STREET AND THE STRIP

A street map of Las Vegas reveals two scales of movement within the gridiron plan: that of Main Street and that of the Strip (Figs. 29, 30). The main street of Las Vegas is Fremont Street, and the earlier of two concentrations of casinos is located along three of four blocks of this street (Fig. 31). The casinos here are bazaarlike in the immediacy to the sidewalk of their clicking and tinkling gambling machines (Fig. 32). The Fremont Street casinos and hotels focus on the railroad depot at the head of the street; here the railroad and main street scales of movement connect. The depot building is now gone, replaced by a hotel, and the bus station is now the busier entrance to town, but the axial focus on the railroad depot from Fremont Street was visual, and possibly sym-

bolic. This contrasts with the Strip, where a second and later development of casinos extends southward to the airport, the jet-scale entrance
to town (Figs. 23, 24, 42, 43, 52, 54).

One's first introduction to Las Vegas architecture is a forebear of
Eero Saarinen's TWA Terminal, which is the local airport building. Beyond this piece of architectural image, impressions are scaled to the car
rented at the airport. Here is the unraveling of the famous Strip itself,
which, as Route 91, connects the airport with the downtown (Fig. 33).

§   SYSTEM AND ORDER ON THE STRIP

The image of the commercial strip is chaos. The order in this landscape is not obvious (Fig. 34). The continuous highway itself and its
systems for turning are absolutely consistent. The median strip accommodates the U-turns necessary to a vehicular promenade for casino
crawlers as well as left turns onto the local street pattern that the Strip
intersects. The curbing allows frequent right turns for casinos and other
commercial enterprises and eases the difficult transitions from highway
to parking. The streetlights function superfluously along many parts of
the Strip that are incidentally but abundantly lit by signs, but their con-
sistency of form and position and their arching shapes begin to identify
by day a continuous space of the highway, and the constant rhythm
contrasts effectively with the uneven rhythms of the signs behind
(Fig. 35).

This counterpoint reinforces the contrast between two types of order
on the Strip: the obvious visual order of street elements and the difficult visual order of buildings and signs. The zone *of* the highway is a
shared order. The zone *off* the highway is an individual order (Fig. 36).
The elements of the highway are civic. The buildings and signs are private. In combination they embrace continuity *and* discontinuity, going
and stopping, clarity *and* ambiguity, cooperation *and* competition, the
community *and* rugged individualism. The system of the highway gives
order to the sensitive functions of exit and entrance, as well as to the
image of the Strip as a sequential whole. It also generates places for individual enterprises to grow and controls the general direction of that
growth. It allows variety and change along its sides and accommodates
the contrapuntal, competitive order of the individual enterprises.

There *is* an order along the sides of the highway. Varieties of activities
are juxtaposed on the Strip: service stations, minor motels, and multimillion-dollar casinos. Marriage chapels ("credit cards accepted") converted from bungalows with added neon-lined steeples are apt to appear
anywhere toward the downtown end. Immediate proximity of related
uses, as on Main Street, where you *walk* from one store to another, is

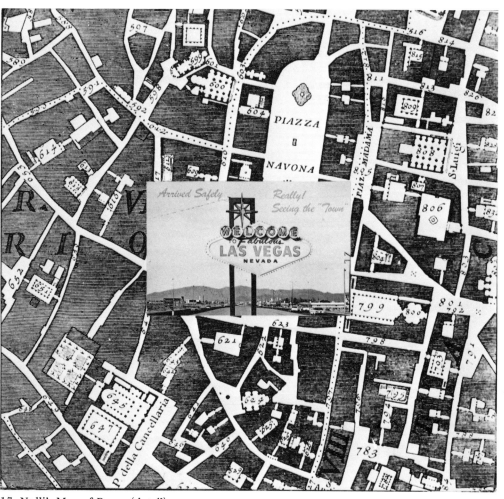

17. Nolli's Map of Rome (detail)

22

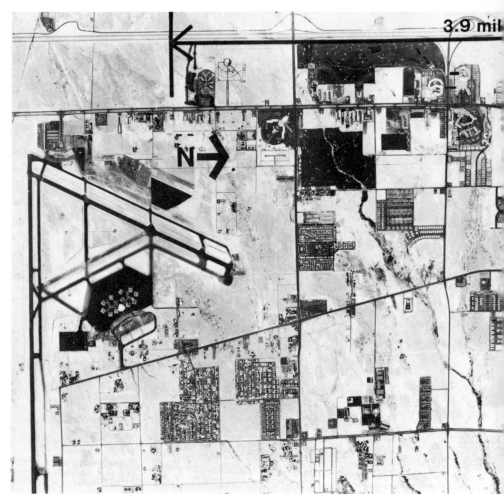

18. Aerial photograph of upper Strip

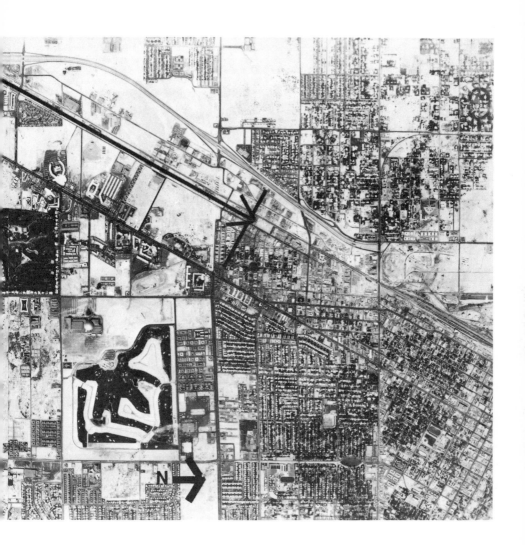

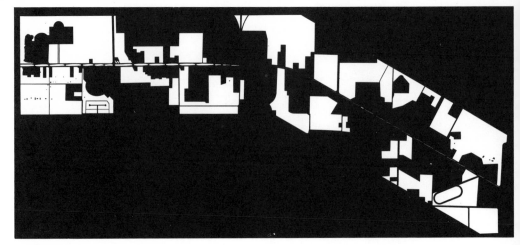

19a. Upper strip, undeveloped land

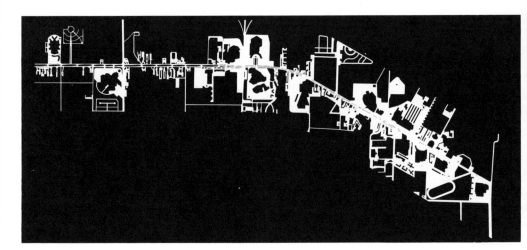

19b. Asphalt

19c. Autos

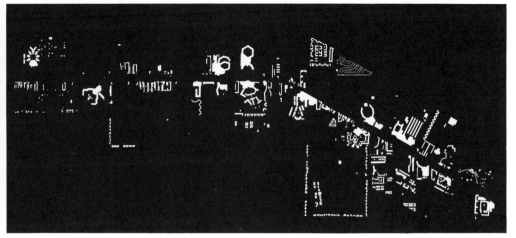

19d. Buildings

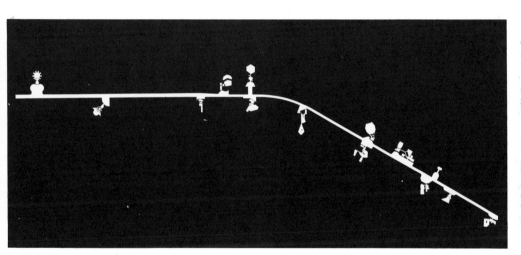

19e. Ceremonial space

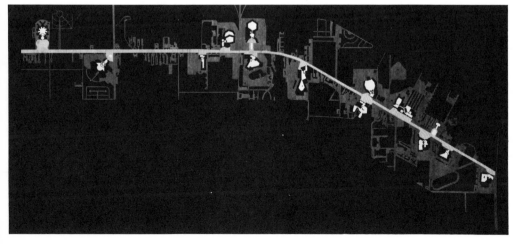

20. Nolli's Las Vegas

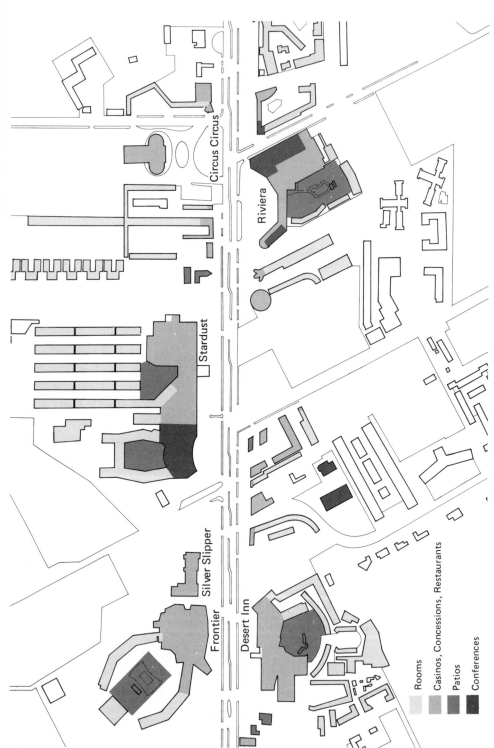

Circus Circus

Riviera

Stardust

Silver Slipper

Frontier

Desert Inn

Rooms

Casinos, Concessions, Restaurants

Patios

Conferences

21. Map of Las Vegas Strip (detail) showing uses within buildings

27

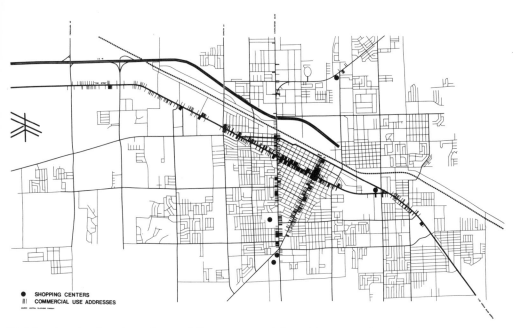

22. Map showing location of ground floor commercial establishments (1961) on three Las Vegas strips

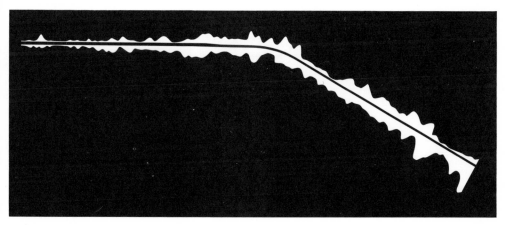

23. Illumination levels on the Strip

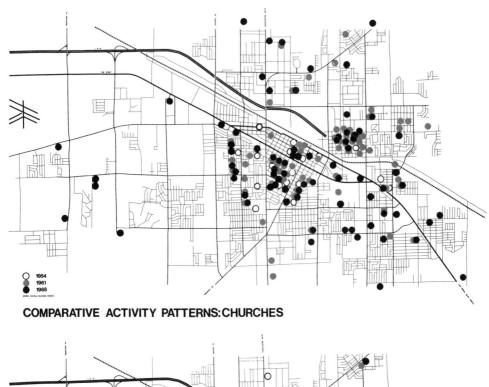

COMPARATIVE ACTIVITY PATTERNS: CHURCHES

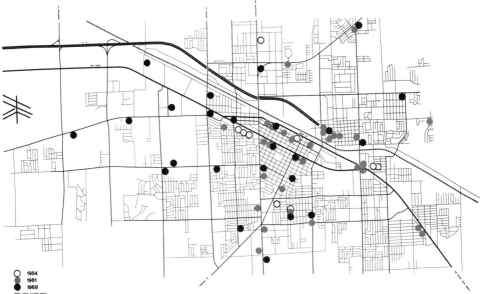

COMPARATIVE ACTIVITY PATTERNS: FOOD STORES

24-27. Maps showing comparative activity patterns: distribution of churches, food stores, wedding chapels, auto rentals

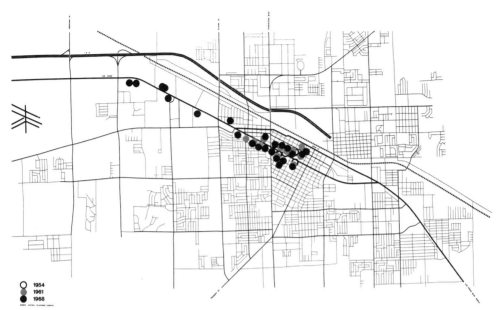

COMPARATIVE ACTIVITY PATTERNS: WEDDING CHAPELS

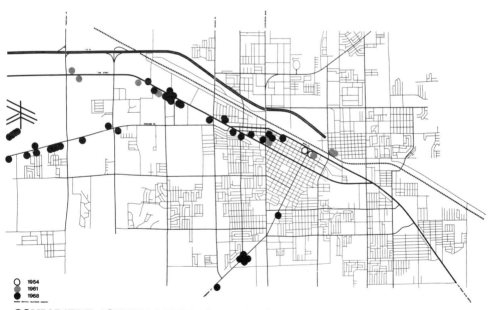

COMPARATIVE ACTIVITY PATTERNS: AUTOMOBILE RENTAL

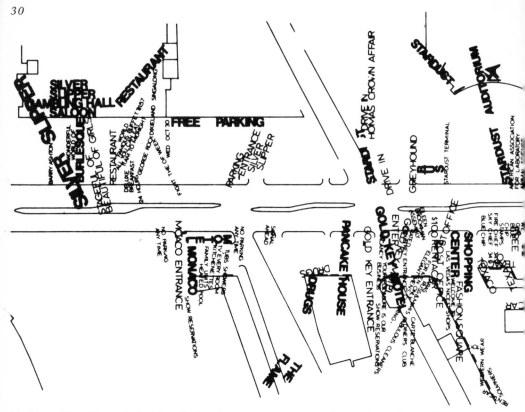

28. Map of Las Vegas Strip (detail) showing every written word seen from the road

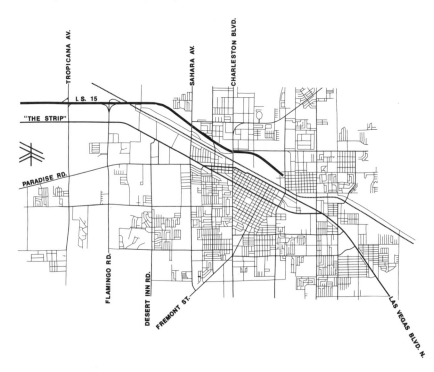

29. Las Vegas street map

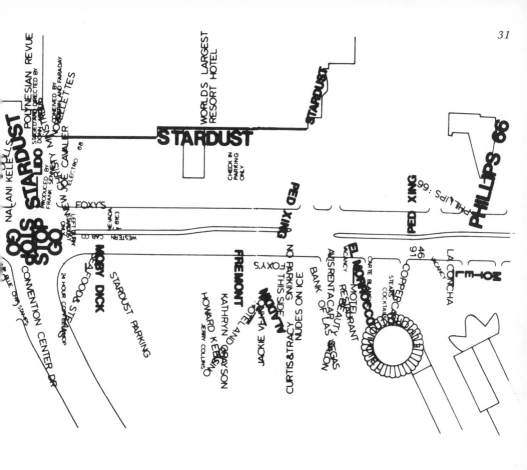

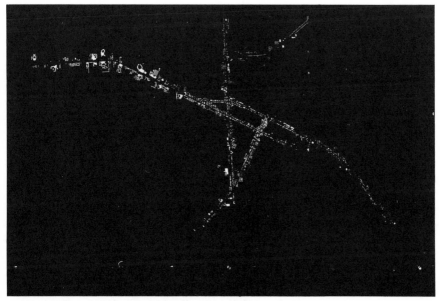

30. Map showing buildings on three Las Vegas strips

31. Fremont Street

33. A detail from an "Edward Ruscha" elevation of the Strip. Tourist maps are made of the Grand Canal and the Rhine showing the route lined by its palaces. Ruscha made one of the Sunset Strip. We imitated his for the Las Vegas Strip.

32. Fremont Street casino entrance

not required along the Strip because interaction is by car and highway. You *drive* from one casino to another even when they are adjacent because of the distance between them, and an intervening service station is not disagreeable.

CHANGE AND PERMANENCE ON THE STRIP

The rate of obsolescence of a sign seems to be nearer to that of an automobile than that of a building. The reason is not physical degeneration but what competitors are doing around you. The leasing system operated by the sign companies and the possibility of total tax write-off may have something to do with it. The most unique, most monumental parts of the Strip, the signs and casino facades, are also the most changeable; it is the neutral, systems-motel structures behind that survive a succession of facelifts and a series of themes up front. The Aladdin Hotel and Casino is Moorish in front and Tudor behind (Fig. 13).

Las Vegas's greatest growth has been since World War II (Figs. 37-40). There are noticeable changes every year: new hotels and signs as well as neon-embossed parking structures replacing on-lot parking on and behind Fremont Street. Like the agglomeration of chapels in a Roman church and the stylistic sequence of piers in a Gothic cathedral, the Golden Nugget casino has evolved over 30 years from a building with a sign on it to a totally sign-covered building (Fig. 41). The Stardust Hotel has engulfed a small restaurant and a second hotel in its expansion and has united the three-piece facade with 600 feet of computer-programmed animated neon.

§ THE ARCHITECTURE OF THE STRIP

It is hard to think of each flamboyant casino as anything but unique, and this is as it should be, because good advertising technique requires the differentiation of the product. However, these casinos have much in common because they are under the same sun, on the same Strip, and perform similar functions; they differ from other casinos—say, on Fremont Street—and from other hotels that are not casinos (Figs. 42, 43).

A typical hotel-casino complex contains a building that is near enough to the highway to be seen from the road across the parked cars, yet far enough back to accommodate driveways, turnarounds, and parking. The parking in front is a token: It reassures the customer but does not obscure the building. It is prestige parking: The customer pays. The bulk of the parking, along the sides of the complex, allows direct access to the hotel yet stays visible from the highway. Parking is seldom at the back. The scales of movement and space of the highway relate to the distances between buildings; because they are far apart, they can be comprehended at high speeds. Front footage on the Strip has not yet reached the value it once had on Main Street, and parking is still an appropriate filler. Big space between buildings is characteristic of the Strip. It is significant that Fremont Street is more photogenic than the Strip. A single postcard can carry a view of the Golden Horseshoe, the Mint Hotel, the Golden Nugget, and the Lucky Casino. A single shot of the Strip is less spectacular; its enormous spaces must be seen as moving sequences (Figs. 44, 45).

The side elevation of the complex is important, because it is seen by approaching traffic from a greater distance and for a longer time than the facade. The rhythmic gables on the long, low, English medieval style, half-timbered motel sides of the Aladdin read emphatically across the parking space (Fig. 46) and through the signs and the giant statue of the neighboring Texaco station, and contrast with the modern Near Eastern flavor of the casino front. Casino fronts on the Strip often inflect in shape and ornament toward the right, to welcome right-lane traffic. Modern styles use a porte cochere that is diagonal in plan. Brazilianoid International styles use free forms.

Service stations, motels, and other simpler types of buildings conform in general to this system of inflection toward the highway through the position and form of their elements. Regardless of the front, the back of the building is styleless, because the whole is turned toward the front and no one sees the back. The gasoline stations parade their universality (Fig. 47). The aim is to demonstrate their similarity to the one at home —your friendly gasoline station. But here they are not the brightest thing in town. This galvanizes them. A motel is a motel anywhere (Fig. 48). But here the imagery is heated up by the need to compete in the surroundings. The artistic influence has spread, and Las Vegas motels have signs like no others. Their ardor lies somewhere between the casinos and the wedding chapels. Wedding chapels, like many urban land uses, are not form-specific (Fig. 49). They tend to be one of a succession of uses a more generalized building type (a bungalow or a store front) may have. But a wedding-chapel style or image is maintained in different types through the use of symbolic ornament in neon, and the activity adapts itself to different inherited plans. Street furniture exists on the Strip as on other city streets, yet it is hardly in evidence.

Beyond the town, the only transition between the Strip and the Mojave Desert is a zone of rusting beer cans (Fig. 50). Within the town, the transition is as ruthlessly sudden. Casinos whose fronts relate so sensitively to the highway turn their ill-kempt backsides toward the local environment, exposing the residual forms and spaces of mechanical equipment and service areas.

34. The order in this landscape is not obvious.

35. Streetlights, upper Strip

36. Upper Strip looking north

37. Las Vegas, August 1905

38. Las Vegas, Fremont Street, 1910

39. Las Vegas, Fremont Street, 1940s

40. Las Vegas, Fremont Street, 1960s

TYPES OF CHANGE

(A) <u>Layerings of Façades & Plans</u>
　　　to expand spatially & stylistically

　　　{ ① Stardust Hotel façade *(by decades)*

　　　　② Gothic Cathedrals *(by generations)*

(B) <u>Competitive Increases in Signs</u>
<u>and Symbols</u>

　　　{ ① Las Vegas Signs

　　　　② San Gimignano Towers

(C) The Strip becomes a Place

　　　{ ① Convention Center & International Hotel

　　　　② the Shopping Center

(D) <u>Building becomes Sign</u>

　　　　① the Golden Nugget

(E) <u>the Evolution of Parking</u>
<u>on "Main Street"</u>

　　　　① The golden nugget
　　　　on Fremont

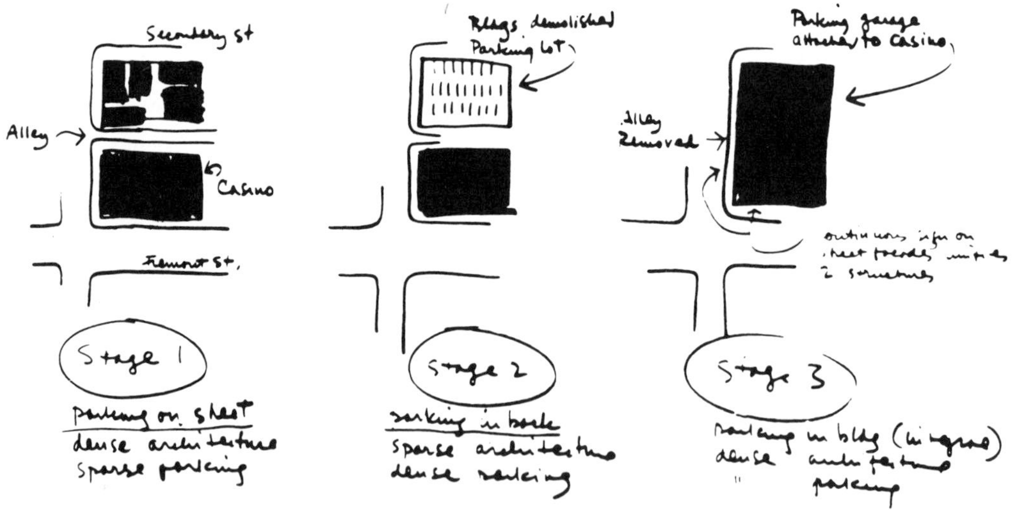

Stage 1
parking on street
dense architecture
sparse parking

Stage 2
parking in back
sparse architecture
dense parking

Stage 3
parking in bldg (in ground)
dense architecture
" parking

Change and Permanence

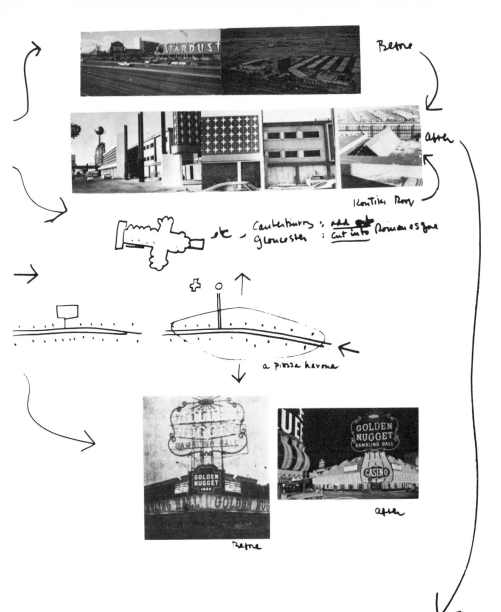

Before

after

Kon Tiki Roof

etc. Canterbury: add
Gloucester: cut into Romanesque

a piazza havona

Before

after

41. Physical change in Las Vegas

42

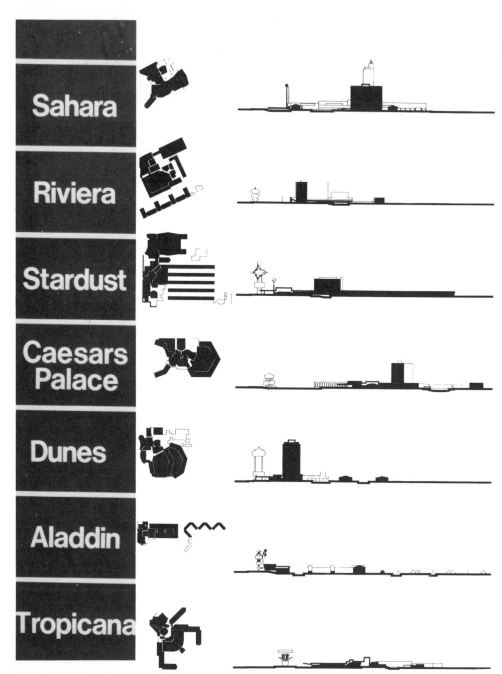

Sahara

Riviera

Stardust

Caesars Palace

Dunes

Aladdin

Tropicana

42. A schedule of Las Vegas Strip hotels: plans, sections, and elements

43. A schedule of Las Vegas Strip hotels: elements, continued

44. Fremont Street hotels and casinos

46. Aladdin Casino and Hotel

45. Portion of a movie
sequence traveling north
on the Strip

46

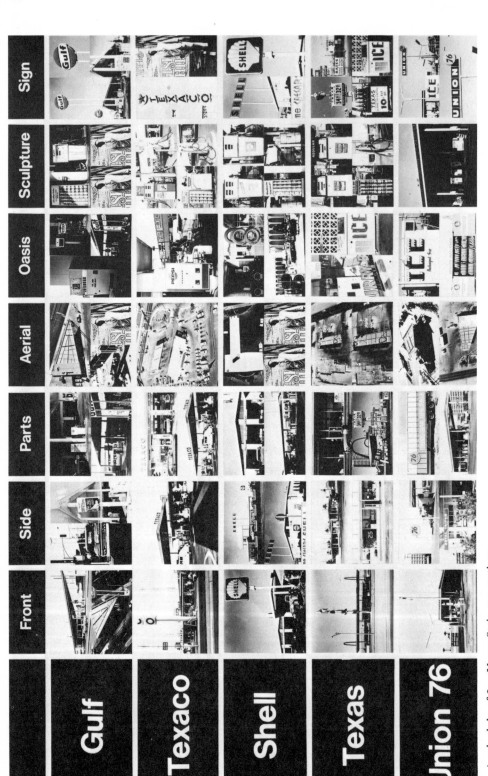

47. A schedule of Las Vegas Strip gas stations

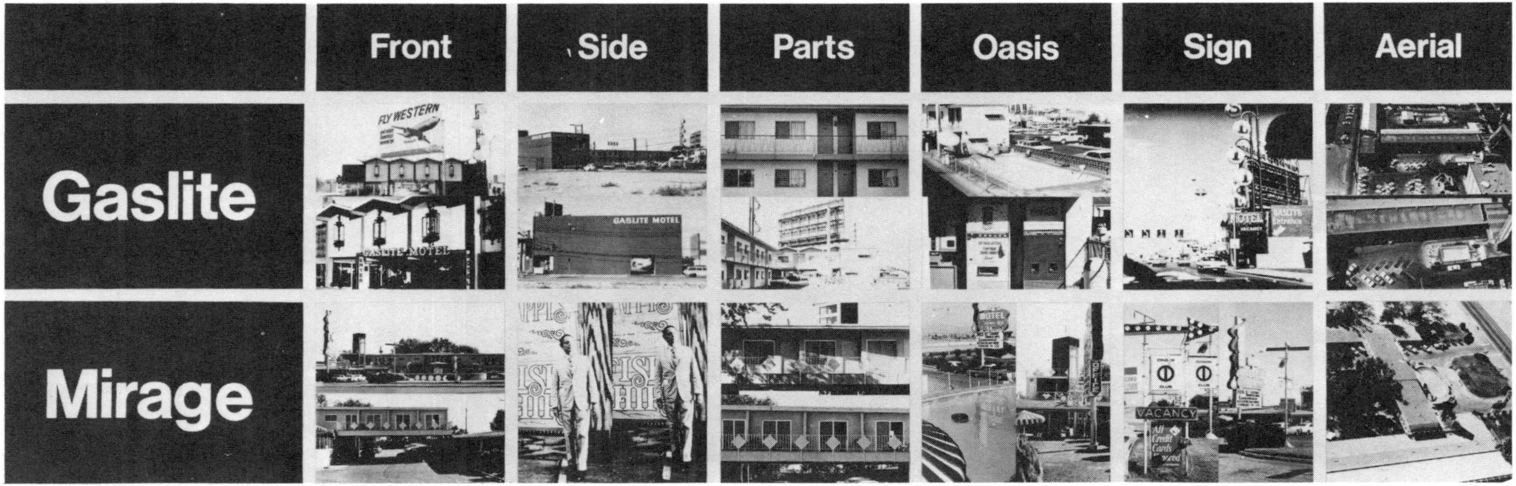

48. A schedule of Las Vegas Strip motels

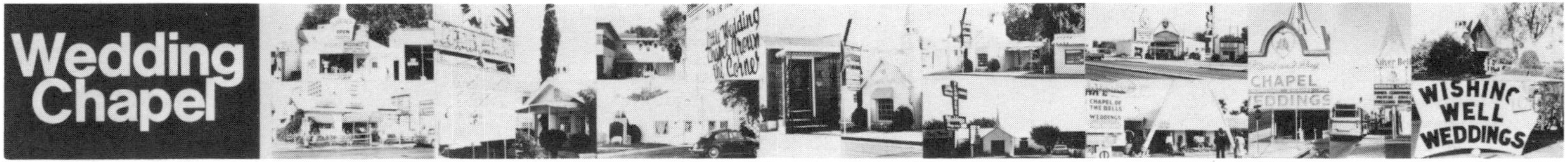

49. A schedule of Las Vegas Strip wedding chapels

50. The Strip from the desert

THE INTERIOR OASIS

If the back of the casino is different from the front for the sake of visual impact in the "autoscape," the inside contrasts with the outside for other reasons. The interior sequence from the front door back progresses from gambling areas to dining, entertainment, and shopping areas, to hotel. Those who park at the side and enter there can interrupt the sequence. But the circulation of the whole focuses on the gambling rooms. In a Las Vegas hotel the registration desk is invariably behind you when you enter the lobby; before you are the gambling tables and machines. The lobby is the gambling room. The interior space and the patio, in their exaggerated separation from the environment, have the quality of an oasis.

§ LAS VEGAS LIGHTING

The gambling room is always very dark; the patio, always very bright. But both are enclosed: The former has no windows, and the latter is open only to the sky. The combination of darkness and enclosure of the gambling room and its subspaces makes for privacy, protection, concentration, and control. The intricate maze under the low ceiling never connects with outside light or outside space. This disorients the occupant in space and time. One loses track of where one is and when it is. Time is limitless, because the light of noon and midnight are exactly the same. Space is limitless, because the artificial light obscures rather than defines its boundaries (Fig. 51). Light is not used to define space. Walls and ceilings do not serve as reflective surfaces for light but are made absorbent and dark. Space is enclosed but limitless, because its edges are dark. Light sources, chandeliers, and the glowing, jukebox-like gambling machines themselves are independent of walls and ceilings. The lighting is antiarchitectural. Illuminated *baldacchini*, more than in all Rome, hover over tables in the limitless shadowy restaurant at the Sahara Hotel.

The artificially lit, air-conditioned interiors complement the glare and heat of the agoraphobic auto-scaled desert. But the interior of the motel patio behind the casino is literally the oasis in a hostile environment (Fig. 52). Whether Organic Modern or Neoclassical Baroque, it contains the fundamental elements of the classic oasis: courts, water, greenery, intimate scale, and enclosed space. Here they are a swimming pool, palms, grass, and other horticultural importations set in a paved court surrounded by hotel suites, balconied or terraced on the court side for privacy. What gives poignance to the beach umbrellas and chaises longues is the vivid, recent memory of the hostile cars poised in the asphalt desert beyond. The pedestrian oasis in the Las Vegas desert is the princely enclosure of the Alhambra, and it is the apotheosis of all the motel courts with swimming pools more symbolic than useful, the plain, low restaurants with exotic interiors, and the pretty shopping malls of the American strip.

§ ARCHITECTURAL MONUMENTALITY AND THE BIG, LOW SPACE

The casino in Las Vegas is big, low space. It is the archetype for all public interior spaces whose heights are diminished for reasons of budget and air conditioning. (The low, one-way-mirrored ceilings also permit outside observation of the gambling rooms.) In the past, volume was governed by structural span; height was relatively easy to achieve. Today, span is easy to achieve, and volume is governed by mechanical and economic limitations on height. But railroad stations, restaurants, and shopping arcades only ten feet high reflect as well a changing attitude to monumentality in our environment. In the past, big spans with their concomitant heights were an ingredient of architectural monumentality (Fig. 53). But our monuments are not the occasional tour de force of an Astrodome, a Lincoln Center, or a subsidized airport. These merely prove that big, high spaces do not automatically make architectural monumentality. We have replaced the monumental space of Pennsylvania Station by a subway above ground, and that of Grand Central Terminal remains mainly through its magnificent conversion to an advertising vehicle. Thus, we rarely achieve architectural monumentality when we try; our money and skill do not go into the traditional monumentality that expressed cohesion of the community through big-scale, unified, symbolic, architectural elements. Perhaps we should admit that our cathedrals are the chapels without the nave and that, apart from theaters and ball parks, the occasional communal space that is big is a space for crowds of anonymous individuals without explicit connection with each other. The big, low mazes of the dark restaurant with alcoves combine being together and yet separate as does the Las Vegas casino. The lighting in the casino achieves a new monumentality for the low space. The controlled sources of artificial and colored light within the dark enclosures expand and unify the space by obscuring its physical limits. You are no longer in the bounded piazza but in the twinkling lights of the city at night.

§ LAS VEGAS STYLES

The Las Vegas casino is a combination form. The complex program of Caesars Palace—one of the grandest—includes gambling, dining and banqueting rooms, nightclubs and auditoria, stores, and a complete hotel. It is also a combination of styles. The front colonnade is San Pietro-Bernini in plan but Yamasaki in vocabulary and scale (Figs. 54, 55); the blue and gold mosaic work is Early Christian tomb of Galla Placidia. (The Baroque symmetry of its prototype precludes an inflection toward the right in this facade.) Beyond and above is a slab in Gio Ponti Pirelli-Baroque, and beyond that, in turn, a low wing in Neoclassical Motel Moderne. Economics has vanquished symmetry in a recent addition. But the new slab and the various styles are integrated by a ubiquity of Ed Stone screens. The landscaping is also eclectic. Within the Piazza San Pietro is the token parking lot. Among the parked cars rise five fountains rather than the two of Carlo Maderno; Villa d'Este cypresses further punctuate the parking environment. Gian de Bologna's *Rape of the Sabine Women* and statues of Venus and David, with slight anatomical exaggerations, grace the area around the porte cochere. Almost bisecting a Venus is an Avis, a sign identifying No. 2's offices on the premises (Figs. 56-58).

The agglomeration of Caesars Palace and of the Strip as a whole approaches the spirit if not the style of the late Roman Forum with its eclectic accumulations. But the sign of Caesars Palace with its Classical, plastic columns is more Etruscan in feeling than Roman (Figs. 59, 60). Although not so high as the Dunes Hotel sign next door or the Shell sign on the other side, its base is enriched by Roman centurions, (Fig. 61) lacquered like Oldenburg hamburgers, who peer over the acres of cars and across their desert empire to the mountains beyond. Their statuesque escorts, carrying trays of fruit, suggest the festivities within and are a background for the family snapshots of Middle Westerners. Massive Miesian light boxes announce square, expensive entertainers such as Jack Benny in 1930s-style marquee lettering appropriate for Benny if not for the Roman architrave it almost ornaments. The light boxes are not in the architrave; they are located off-center on the columns in order to inflect toward the highway and the parking.

§ LAS VEGAS SIGNS

Signs inflect toward the highway even more than buildings. The big sign—independent of the building and more or less sculptural or pictorial—inflects by its position, perpendicular to and at the edge of the highway, by its scale, and sometimes by its shape. The sign of the Aladdin Hotel and Casino seems to bow toward the highway through the inflection in its shape (Fig. 62). It also is three dimensional, and parts of it revolve. The sign at the Dunes Hotel is more chaste: It is only two dimensional, and its back echoes its front, but it is an erection 22 stories high that pulsates at night (Fig. 63). The sign for The Mint Hotel on Route 91 at Fremont Street inflects toward the Casino several blocks away. Signs in Las Vegas use mixed media—words, pictures, and sculpture—to persuade and inform. A sign is, contradictorily, for day and night. The same sign works as polychrome sculpture in the sun and as black silhouette against the sun; at night it is a source of light. It revolves by day and becomes a play of lights at night (Figs. 64-67). It contains scales for close-up and for distance (Fig. 68). Las Vegas has the longest sign in the world, the Thunderbird, and the highest, the Dunes. Some signs are hardly distinguishable at a distance from the occasional high-rise hotels along the Strip. The sign of the Pioneer Club on Fremont Street talks. Its cowboy, 60 feet high, says "Howdy Pardner" every 30 seconds. The big sign at the Aladdin Hotel has spawned a little sign with similar proportions to mark the entrance to the parking. "But such signs!" says Tom Wolfe. "They soar in shapes before which the existing vocabulary of art history is helpless. I can only attempt to supply names—Boomerang Modern, Palette Curvilinear, Flash Gordon Ming-Alert Spiral, McDonald's Hamburger Parabola, Mint Casino Elliptical, Miami Beach Kidney."[3] Buildings are also signs. At night on Fremont Street, whole buildings are illuminated but not through reflection from spotlights; they are made into sources of light by closely spaced neon tubes. Amid the diversity, the familiar Shell and Gulf signs stand out like friendly beacons in a foreign land. But in Las Vegas they reach three times higher into the air than at your local service station to meet the competition of the casinos.

§ INCLUSION AND THE DIFFICULT ORDER

Henri Bergson called disorder an order we cannot see. The emerging order of the Strip is a complex order. It is not the easy, rigid order of the urban renewal project or the fashionable "total design" of the megastructure. It is, on the contrary, a manifestation of an opposite direction in architectural theory: Broadacre City—a travesty of Broadacre City, perhaps, but a kind of vindication of Frank Lloyd Wright's predictions for the American landscape. The commercial strip within the urban sprawl is, of course, Broadacre City with a difference. Broadacre City's easy, motival order identified and unified its vast spaces and separate buildings at the scale of the omnipotent automobile. Each building, without doubt, was to be designed by the Master or by his Taliesin Fellowship, with no room for honky-tonk improvisations. An easy control would be exercised over similar elements within the universal, Usonian vocabulary to the exclusion, certainly, of commercial vulgarities. But the order of the Strip *includes*; it includes at all levels, from the mixture of seemingly incongruous land uses to the mixture of

3. Tom Wolfe, *The Kandy-Colored Tangerine-Flake Streamline Baby* (New York: Noonday Press, 1966), p. 8.

seemingly incongruous advertising media plus a system of neo-Organic or neo-Wrightian restaurant motifs in Walnut Formica (Fig. 69). It is not an order dominated by the expert and made easy for the eye. The moving eye in the moving body must work to pick out and interpret a variety of changing, juxtaposed orders, like the shifting configurations of a Victor Vasarely painting (Fig. 70). It is the unity that "maintains, but only just maintains, a control over the clashing elements which compose it. Chaos is very near; its nearness, but its avoidance, gives . . . force."[4]

§ IMAGE OF LAS VEGAS: INCLUSION AND
ALLUSION IN ARCHITECTURE

Tom Wolfe used Pop prose to suggest powerful images of Las Vegas. Hotel brochures and tourist handouts suggest others (Fig. 71). J. B. Jackson, Robert Riley, Edward Ruscha, John Kouwenhoven, Reyner Banham, and William Wilson have elaborated on related images. For the architect or urban designer, comparisons of Las Vegas with others of the world's "pleasure zones" (Fig. 72)—with Marienbad, the Alhambra, Xanadu, and Disneyland, for instance—suggest that essential to the imagery of pleasure-zone architecture are lightness, the quality of being an oasis in a perhaps hostile context, heightened symbolism, and the ability to engulf the visitor in a new role: for three days one may imagine oneself a centurion at Caesars Palace, a ranger at the Frontier, or a jetsetter at the Riviera rather than a salesperson from Des Moines, Iowa, or an architect from Haddonfield, New Jersey.

However, there are didactic images more important than the images of recreation for us to take home to New Jersey and Iowa: one is the Avis with the Venus; another, Jack Benny under a classical pediment with Shell Oil beside him, or the gasoline station beside the multimillion-dollar casino. These show the vitality that may be achieved by an architecture of inclusion or, by contrast, the deadness that results from too great a preoccupation with tastefulness and total design. The Strip shows the value of symbolism and allusion in an architecture of vast space and speed and proves that people, even architects, have fun with architecture that reminds them of something else, perhaps of harems or the Wild West in Las Vegas, perhaps of the nation's New England forebears in New Jersey. Allusion and comment, on the past or present or on our great commonplaces or old clichés, and inclusion of the everyday in the environment, sacred and profane—these are what are lacking in present-day Modern architecture. We can learn about them from Las Vegas as have other artists from their own profane and stylistic sources.

4. August Heckscher, *The Public Happiness* (New York: Atheneum Publishers, 1962), p. 289.

51. Caesars Palace tourist brochure

52. Caesars Palace oasis

OLD
monumentality

NEW
monumentality

<u>The nave</u>

<u>The chapels without the nave</u>

The big
1. HIGH
2. LIT and WINDOWED
3. OPEN
4. SPACE
5. UNCLUTTERED

The big
1. LOW
2. GLITTERING-in-the-DARK
3. ENCLOSED
4. MAZE of
5. ALCOVES and
6. FURNITURE

for communal crowds

for separate people

1. High for monumentality

2. Lit and windowed: natural & simulated daylight falls on walls to clarify the great architecture

3. Open: to let natural light in and lately to integrate the inside & outside

4. Space: spaciousness for communal crowds

5. Uncluttered: don't clutter up the great architecture.

1. Low for economy of air conditioning

2. glittering-in-the-Dark: perimeters dark in value, absorbent in texture to obscure extent and character of the architectural enclosure. glittering light sources - mainly ornamental - and recessed ceiling spots to light people and furniture and not architecture.

3. Enclosed to exclude the outside to engender a different style and role inside

4. Maze for crowds of anonymous individuals without explicit connections with each other

5. Alcoves: people are together and yet separate

6. Furniture: objects and symbols dominate architecture.

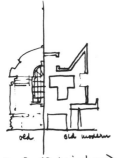

old   old modern

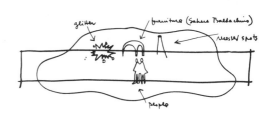

glitter   furniture (Sahara Baldachino)   recessed spots

people

part of Topic 8 (Building types)

THE ROADSIDE INTERIOR

53. Architectural monumentality and the roadside interior

54. Caesars Palace

The grandeur that was Rome...

I, CAESAR . . . command your attention to beauty and wonders beyond even the wildest dreams of any Roman Emperor! Truly a Palace of Pleasure! In the vital heart of pulsating Las Vegas this exciting and lush oasis is breathtaking to behold . . . lavish with gleaming statuary, gorgeous gardens and fabulous fountains! A mighty retinue of toga-clad palace attendants eagerly await your every summons! Come, indulge yourself!

55. Caesars Palace tourist brochure

STATUARY

AT

CAESARS PALACE

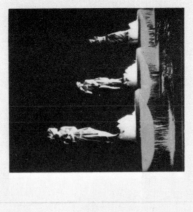

CAESARS PALACE takes pride in presenting these magnificently achieved Carrara marble statues, imported from Italy and representing some of the greatest art treasures of modern man.

In tribute to a Roman patron Michaelangelo once observed that the artist and sculptor created their art works to sate their own needs and hungers, but that those who glorified the works of others by displaying these treasures were the most noble of all men, since they were perpetuating a culture for all the world.

The brilliant contemporary sculptor, Sir Henry Moore, said: "Sculpture is an art of free space. It needs daylight, sunlight. Nature seems to be its best setting..." In recognition of this, the CAESARS PALACE landscaping and architecture were designed to achieve the most effective and beautiful setting for these great works of art.

The statues on display at CAESARS PALACE are carved in sparkling white Carrara marble, cut from the mountain in Italy from which Michaelangelo took his stone.

CAESARS PALACE

3570 LAS VEGAS BLVD SOUTH   LAS VEGAS, NEVADA 87107

VENUS DE MEDICI, by Cleomenes, carved about 100 B.C., is an extraordinary example of the Hellenistic art. The inspiration for this famous statue of the Goddess attempting to cover her nakedness was the Venus of Cnidus, and was commissioned by the Medicis family. The Medicis ruled the city of Florence during the days of the Renaissance, a period of artistic splendor and achievement, and they subsidized a number of talented painters and sculptors. This Venus now stands in Galleria Uffizi, in Florence, Italy.

VICTORY AT SAMOTHRACE, by an unknown sculptor, was created about 300 B.C. This winged figure of victory, discovered in the Aegean island of Samothrace, was originally designed for the prow of the ship sailed by Pliiocretes. The nobility and beauty of this monumental art work is honored by being given a place of special distinction in the famous Louvre Museum, in Paris, France.

56. Caesars Palace tourist brochure

57-58. Caesars Palace signs and statuary

59. Caesars Palace sign

0. Piranesi's Pantheon/Caesars Palace sign

1. Caesars Palace centurions

Las Vegas signs and buildings

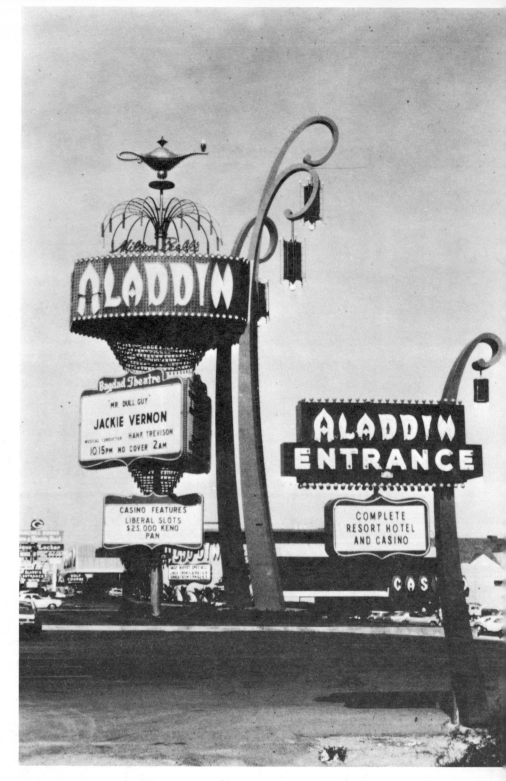

62. Aladdin signs

63. Dunes hotel and signs

66

64-67. Stardust sign

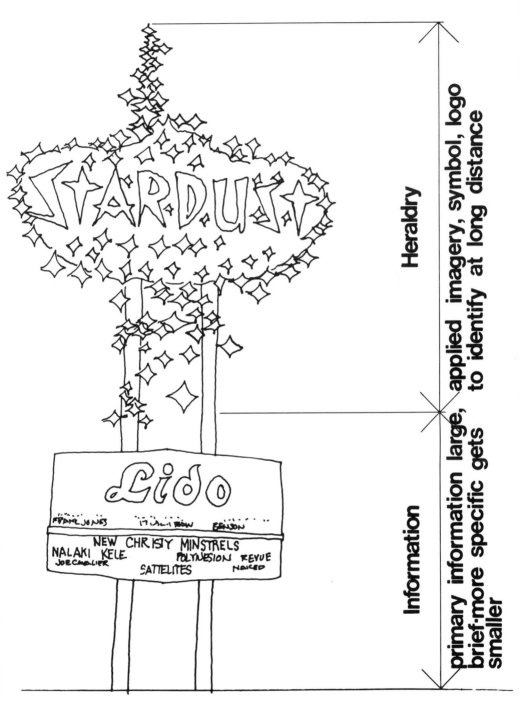

68. Physiognomy of a typical casino sign

Concerning Strip Beautification

a message to the Strip Beautification Commission

<u>Not</u> the image of the Champs Elysées

    trees block views of signs
    grass medians are hard to maintain
    lots of greenery and water raise humidity level
      of city

Best things strip has are signs & architecture

Gas stations are all right
    their standard image plays against the unique
      architecture of the hotels
    (in fact the gas stations are tasteful in
      comparison with the hotels)

Model should be the Near East:
    Tile
    Mosaics
    Maximum effect with a minimum amount of water
  + Electro-graphics

The Median of The Strip should be <u>paved in gold</u>

Remember the floors of the parking lots

69. A message to the Strip Beautification Committee

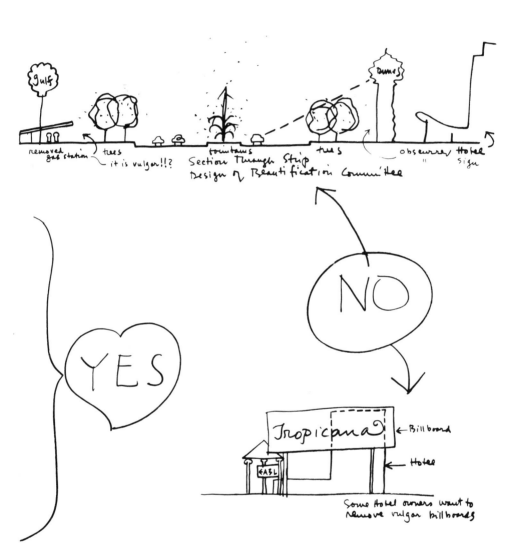

Section Through Strip
Design of Beautification Committee

removed gas station   trees   it is vulgar!!?   fountains   trees   observers   Hotel sign

YES

NO

Tropicana ← Billboard

← Hotel

Some Hotel owners want to remove vulgar billboards

71. Las Vegas tourist brochure

70. Painting by Victor Vasarely

PLEASURE ZONES
CHARACTERISTICS

	MIAMI BEACH
	MARIENBAD
	ATLANTIC CITY
	XANADU
	SHOPPING CENTER
LIGHT ARCHITECTURE lacy and diminutive Yamasaki modern	BATH
	ALHAMBRA
	DISNEYLAND
	PERSIAN GARDEN
	WORLDS FAIR
	HADRIAN'S VILLA
IN A HOSTILE CONTEXT, THE OASIS desert ocean parking lots fortifications	LAS VEGAS
	MIAMI BEACH
	MARIENBAD
	ATLANTIC CITY
	XANADU
SYMBOLIC ARCHITECTURE AND GARDENS late periods erotic arcadian Romantic etc.	SHOPPING CENTER
	BATH
	ALHAMBRA
	DISNEYLAND
	PERSIAN GARDEN
	WORLDS FAIR
	HADRIAN'S VILLA
ROLE PLAYING eclectic resort hotels of Morris Lapidus Versailles	LAS VEGAS
	MIAMI BEACH

72. A comparative analysis of Pleasure Zones

Pop artists have shown the value of the old cliché used in a new context to achieve a new meaning—the soup can in the art gallery—to make the common uncommon. And in literature, Eliot and Joyce display, according to Poirier, "an extraordinary vulnerability . . . to the idioms, rhythms, artifacts, associated with certain urban environments or situations. The multitudinous styles of *Ulysses* are so dominated by them that there are only intermittent sounds of Joyce in the novel and no extended passage certifiably in his as distinguished from a mimicked style."[5] Poirier refers to this as the "decreative impulse."[6] Eliot himself speaks of Joyce's doing the best he can "with the material at hand."[7] Perhaps a fitting requiem for the irrelevant works of Art that are today's descendants of a once meaningful Modern architecture are Eliot's lines in "East Coker":[8]

That was a way of putting it—not very satisfactory:
A periphrastic study in a worn-out poetical fashion,
Leaving one still with the intolerable wrestle
With words and meanings. The poetry does not matter. . . .

5. Richard Poirier, "T. S. Eliot," p. 20.

6. Ibid., p. 21.

7. T. S. Eliot, *The Complete Poems and Plays, 1909-1950* (New York: Harcourt, Brace and Company, 1958), p. 125.

8. T. S. Eliot, *Four Quartets* (New York: Harcourt, Brace and Company, 1943), p. 13.

STUDIO NOTES

§ A SIGNIFICANCE FOR A&P PARKING LOTS, OR LEARNING FROM LAS VEGAS: A STUDIO RESEARCH PROBLEM

School of Art and Architecture, Yale University, Fall 1968

Joint authors:
Robert Venturi
Denise Scott Brown
Steven Izenour

Students:
Ralph Carlson
Tony Farmer
Ron Filson
Glen Hodges
Peter Hoyt
Charles Korn
John Kranz
Peter Schlaifer
Peter Schmitt
Dan Scully
Doug Southworth
Martha Wagner
Tony Zunino

The studio programs and work topics were designed by Denise Scott Brown. Portions of them are quoted in these notes. Excerpts from writings by students have their names appended.

§ COMMERCIAL VALUES AND COMMERCIAL METHODS

This has been a technical studio. We are evolving new tools: analytical tools for understanding new space and form, and graphic tools for represent-

§ See material under the corresponding heading in Part I.

ing them. Don't bug us for lack of social concern; we are trying to train ourselves to offer *socially* relevant skills.

§ SYMBOL IN SPACE BEFORE FORM IN SPACE: LAS VEGAS AS A COMMUNICATION SYSTEM

WELCOME TO FABULOUS LAS VEGAS, FREE ASPIRIN—ASK US ANYTHING, VACANCY, GAS.

All cities communicate messages—functional, symbolic, and persuasive—to people as they move about. Las Vegas signs hit you at the California border and before you land at the airport. On the Strip three message systems exist: the *heraldic*—the signs—dominates (Fig. 1); the *physiognomic*, the messages given by the faces of the buildings—the continuous balconies and regularly spaced picture windows of the Dunes saying HOTEL (Fig. 3) and the suburban bungalows converted to chapels by the addition of a steeple (Fig. 4)—and the *locational*—service stations are found on corner lots, the casino is in front of the hotel, and the ceremonial valet parking is in front of the casino. All three message systems are closely interrelated on the Strip. Sometimes they are combined, as when the facade of a casino becomes one big sign (Fig. 5) or the shape of the building reflects its name, and the sign, in turn, reflects the shape. Is the sign the building or the building the sign?

These relationships, and combinations between signs and buildings, between architecture and symbolism, between form and meaning, between driver and the roadside are deeply relevant to architecture today and have been discussed at length by several writers. But they have not been studied in detail or as an overall system. The students of urban perception and "imageability" have ignored them, and there is some evidence that the Strip would confound their theories. How is it that in spite of "noise" from competing signs we do in fact find what we want on the Strip? Also, we have no good graphic tools for depicting the Strip as message giver. How can the visual importance of the Stardust sign be mapped at 1 inch to 100 feet?

§ THE ARCHITECTURE OF PERSUASION

In *The View From the Road.* Appleyard, Lynch, and Myer describe the driving experience as "a sequence played to the eyes of a captive, somewhat fearful, but partially inattentive audience, whose vision is filtered and directed forward."[1]

Movement perception along a road is within a structural order of constant elements—the road, sky, lamppost spacing, and yellow stripes. A person can orient to this, while the rest just happens! Lynch found that more than half the objects sighted along a road by both drivers and passengers are seen straight ahead and narrowly to the sides, as if with blinders (Fig. 11). (That is why the sign must be big and must be along the road.) About one-third of the attention is off to the immediate sides. Attention is also more focused on "moving" objects than on "stable" ones, except when the observer passes a visual barrier and, in order to reorient, surveys a new landscape. Speed is the determinant of focal angle, both for driver and passengers. Increases of speed narrow the focal angle with a resulting visual shift from detail to generality; attention shifts to points of decision. The body sensations of speed are few in a car. We depend upon vision for our perception of speed. Objects that pass overhead greatly increase the sense of speed.

Does Las Vegas make any attempt to control speed—slow down, therefore see more detail, therefore buy? (Daniel Scully and Peter Schmitt)

§ VAST SPACE IN THE HISTORICAL TRADITION AND AT THE A&P

The Las Vegas Strip eludes our concepts of urban form and space, ancient or modern. It has as little to do with Haussmann as

1. Donald Appleyard, Kevin Lynch, and John R. Myer, *The View From the Road* (Cambridge, Mass.: The M.I.T. Press, 1964), p. 5.

with Ville Radieuse, with Ebenezer Howard as with the Metabolists, with Lynch as with Camillo Sitte or Ian Nairn. Frank Lloyd Wright would have considered it a travesty of Broadacre City, and Maki would probably find it a travesty of "group form." Perhaps Patrick Geddes might have understood and J. B. Jackson is very much attuned to it.

Although its buildings suggest a number of historical styles, its urban spaces owe nothing to historical space. Las Vegas space is neither contained and enclosed like medieval space nor classically balanced and proportioned like Renaissance space nor swept up in a rhythmically ordered movement like Baroque space, nor does it flow like Modern space around freestanding urban space makers.

It is something else again. But what? Not chaos, but a new spatial order relating the automobile and highway communication in an architecture which abandons pure form in favor of mixed media. Las Vegas space is so different from the docile spaces for which our analytical and conceptual tools were evolved that we need new concepts and theories to handle it.

One way of understanding the new form and space is to compare it with the old and the different. Compare Las Vegas with Ville Radieuse and Haussmann's Paris; compare the Strip with a medieval market street (Figs. 8, 12); compare Fremont Street, a shopping center, and the pilgrims' way through Rome. Compare a form that "just grew" with its designed equivalent and with "group forms" from other cultures.

Another way of understanding the new form is to describe carefully and then analyze what is there and, from an understanding of the city as is, to evolve new theories and concepts of form more suited to twentieth-century realities and therefore more useful as conceptual tools in design and planning. This approach provides a way out of the CIAM grid. But how does one describe new form and space using techniques derived from the old? What techniques can represent the 60mph form and space of the Strip? How does its desert site affect Las Vegas form and space?

Do Las Vegas public and institutional buildings show any influences from its recreational architecture?

§ MAPS OF LAS VEGAS (FIGS. 18-27, 71)

The representation techniques learned from architecture and planning impede our understanding of Las Vegas. They are static where it is dynamic, contained where it is open, two-dimensional where it is three-dimensional—how do you show the Aladdin sign meaningfully in plan, section, and elevation, or show the Golden Slipper on a land-use plan? Architectural techniques are suitable for large, broad objects in space, like buildings, but not for thin, intense objects, like signs; planning techniques are able to depict activity (land use), but in excessively general categories, for the ground floor only, and without intensity.

We need techniques for abstracting, for example, to represent "twin phenomena" or to demonstrate concepts and generalized schema—an archetypal casino or a piece of the urban fabric—rather than specific buildings. The pretty photographs that we and other tourists made in Las Vegas are not enough.

How do you *distort* these to draw out a meaning for a designer? How do you differentiate on a plan between form that is to be specifically built as shown and that which is, within constraints, allowed to happen? How do you represent the Strip as perceived by Mr. A. rather than as a piece of geometry? How do you show quality of light—or qualities of form—in plan at 1 inch to 100 feet? How do you show fluxes and flows, or seasonal variation, or change with time?

LAS VEGAS AS A PATTERN OF
ACTIVITIES

A city is a set of intertwined activities that form a pattern on the land. The Las Vegas Strip is not a chaotic sprawl but a set of activities whose pattern, as with other cities, depends on the technology of movement and communication and the economic value of land. We term it sprawl, because it is a new pattern we have not yet understood. The aim here is for us as designers to derive an understanding of this new pattern.

The questions are: How can the traditional city planning methods for depicting activity patterns (land-use and transportation maps) be adapted to a city such as Las Vegas? How can they be made useful as inspiration sources and design tools for urban designers? What other methods are there for coming to an understanding of the city as an activity system?

In search of answers, we shall experiment with different techniques for representing the following:

1. Las Vegas and the Strip as phenomena in the space economy, national and local.
2. Land use and intensity of use for the region in general and the Strip in detail.
3. The linkages between activities on and around the Strip.
4. Movement and stopping systems for auto, transit, pedestrian, rail, and air for the region and for pedestrian, transit, and auto for the Strip.
5. Volume and flow of different types of traffic at different time periods.
6. The relation between activities and movement at different scales along the Strip.
7. The Strip as recreation system, a promenade.

These studies will give us a broad understanding of why things are where they are in Las Vegas.

§ MAIN STREET AND THE STRIP

On Fremont Street the casinos are part of the sidewalk (Figs. 31-33). On the Strip the public space goes right through the casinos and into the patios beyond, where the relation between public open space and private suites is mediated by a set of sensitive devices. Even the parking lots, which in other cities have about the same public significance as the bathroom corridor (that is, they *are* public, but you would rather not notice them), are here ritualized and given a ceremonial function. The relation between public space, public-private space, and private space is as intricate and intriguing as that of the Rome of the Counter-Reformation (Figs. 23, 24, 42, 43, 52, 54).

§ SYSTEM AND ORDER ON THE STRIP: "TWIN PHENOMENA"

Aldo van Eyck has defined what others might call polar opposites—inside and outside, public and private, unique and general—as "twin phenomena," because these pairs are inextricably intertwined at every level in the city.

Differences between the blazing outside and the cool, dark inside are poignantly strong in Las Vegas; yet they are counter-crossed by the domesticated "outside" inside the patio and by the night-sky lighting of the casino lounges. Day is negated inside the casinos, and night is negated on the Strip. The signs are, contradictorily, for day *and* night.

The casinos flaunt their uniqueness yet are backed by generalized systematized motel space behind. They are set off by the gasoline stations that use their standard, national designs but make their signs uniquely high. The street lighting and road signs are rigidly systematic in contrast with the signs of persuasion that shout their gorgeous cacophony but hide their constraining order (Figs. 35, 36). Some Strip establishments, such as casinos and wedding chapels, are generators, and others, such as motels and gasoline stations, benefit from the market generated.

§ THE ARCHITECTURE OF THE STRIP: COMPILING A PATTERN BOOK (FIGS. 42-49)

To find the system behind the flamboyance, we devised schedules of individual building parts—floors, walls, gas pumps, parking lots, plans, elevation (front, back, and side)—for different building types and for portions of the street. These parts can then be reassembled as a two-dimensional graph for each building type with buildings on the X axis and parts of buildings on the Y axis. Reading across we have one building; reading down one column, all elevations of that building type on the Strip; and on the diagonal, a prototypical building (Figs. 42, 43).

GASOLINE STATIONS (FIG. 47)

The client: The real estate department of the oil company. Handles site acquisition, construction and coordination, financing, and so forth.

The site: Determined by the traffic count, cost of land, and competition. Frontage generally determines cost—average 150 feet.

The building: Two or three service bays, facing the front; the office; storage space; customer services—"travel center," vending machines, rest rooms, and so forth.

The styling: Pressures from the beautification people and local zoning boards; Mobil's "modern" box, Shell's "ranch house," and the universal "Colonial" (it's just like your suburban house, except it has pumps in front); use of residential materials—wood, brick, stone; a trend toward standardized form where the building becomes a sign.

The signs: Three orders of magnitude: one sign for great distances (freeway scale); one sign for approach distances (feeder road); the building or sign canopy for close-up.

The lighting: Says station is open; lighting crucial at entrance,

exit, and pumps. Oil companies want the source of light visible for maximum impact, resist indirect lighting; big problems with bugs and with zoning boards.

The service area: Pumps and oil displays; canopy provides protection from the sun and bad weather and acts as a sign (Mobil's circle or Phillips' soaring V). Must be fully visible from the service bays in the station, because most stations are one- or two-man operations. There must be plenty of room to maneuver in order to prevent collisions with the pumps and equipment.

"For the average citizen there are some simple tests which will tell him when we have passed from incantation to practical action on the environment. Restriction of auto use in the large cities will be one. Another will be when the billboards, the worst and most nearly useless excrescence of industrial civilization, are removed from the highways. . . . My own personal test, for what it may be worth, concerns the gasoline service station. This is the most repellent piece of architecture of the past two thousand years. There are far more of them than are needed. Usually they are filthy. Their merchandise is hideously packaged and garishly displayed. They are uncontrollably addicted to great strings of ragged little flags. Protecting them is an ominous coalition of small businessmen and large. The stations

should be excluded entirely from most streets and highways. Where allowed, they should be franchised to limit the number, and there should be stern requirements as to architecture, appearance, and general reticence. When we begin on this (and similar roadside commerce), I will think that we are serious."
—John Kenneth Galbraith[2]

MOTELS (FIG. 48)

The site: Determined by traffic count, access to freeways, frontage costs, easy visibility; office and restaurant nearest road; meeting rooms (to draw the businessman); bedrooms away from road, adjacent to parking and grouped about a pool, patio, and so forth.

The buildings: Office and canopy with temporary parking; restaurant with parking; convention facilities; bedrooms near parking and connected by covered walkways to other facilities; the standard room size is 14 feet wide by 27, 24, or 21 feet long. Enter off a double-loaded corridor, luggage rack, closet and shelf space on one side; dressing room with sink and bathroom on other; then bed-sitting room; large sliding glass window to patio, balcony, pool; TV opposite the bed; luggage rack, desk, and TV counter in one contin-

2. John Kenneth Galbraith, "To My New Friends in the Affluent Society— Greetings," *Life* (March 27, 1970), p. 20.

uous counter top; generally one or two double beds with assorted remote controls in the headboard.

The styling: Inside, it avoids the all-bedroom look (just like home but a bit more luxurious); outside, the basic components are standardized so that the building becomes the sign, like the Howard Johnson and the Holiday Inn. (Peter Hoyt)

§ LAS VEGAS LIGHTING

Las Vegas daylight, like Greek daylight, makes the polychrome temples stand out proud and clear in the desert. This is a quality hard to catch on film. No photographs of the Acropolis do it justice. And Las Vegas is better known for its night light than its daylight.

§ ARCHITECTURAL MONUMENTALITY AND THE BIG, LOW SPACE: THE FONTAINEBLEAU

"To get into the dining room you walk up three steps, open a pair of doors and walk out on a platform, and then walk down three steps. Now the dining room is at exactly the same level as my lobby, but as they walk up they reach the platform. I've got soft light lighting this thing up, and before they're seated, they are on stage as if they had been cast for the part. Everybody's look-

ing at them; they're looking at everybody else."
—Morris Lapidus[3]

§ LAS VEGAS STYLES

Miami Moroccan, International Jet Set Style; Arte Moderne Hollywood Orgasmic, Organic Behind; Yamasaki Bernini cum Roman Orgiastic; Niemeyer Moorish; Moorish Tudor (Arabian Knights); Bauhaus Hawaiian.

"People are looking for illusions; they don't want the world's realities. And, I asked, where do I find this world of illusion? Where are their tastes formulated? Do they study it in school? Do they go to museums? Do they travel in Europe? Only one place—the movies. They go to the movies. The hell with everything else."
—Morris Lapidus[4]

§ LAS VEGAS SIGNS (FIGS. 62-68)

The time has arrived for a scholar to write a doctoral dissertation on signs. He or she would need literary as well as artistic acumen, because the same reason that makes signs Pop Art (the need for high-speed communication with maximum meaning) makes them Pop literature as

3. Morris Lapidus, quoted in *Progressive Architecture* (September 1970), p. 122.

4. Ibid., p. 120.

well. For example, this one from Philadelphia:

O. R. LUMPKIN. BODYBUILDERS. FENDERS STRAIGHTENED. WRECKS OUR SPECIALTY. WE TAKE THE DENT OUT OF ACCIDENT.

We shall be analyzing and categorizing the signs of Las Vegas by content and form, by function (night and day) and location, as well as by size, color, structure, and method of construction, trying to understand what makes the "Las Vegas style" in signs and what we can learn from them about an impure architecture of form and symbols.

A stylistic analysis of Las Vegas signs would trace the influence of the greats (the designers in YESCO) through to the minor architecture of wedding chapels and sauna baths, compare the national and general sign imagery of the gasoline stations with the unique and specific symbolic imagery of the casinos, and follow the influence patterns back and forth between artists and sign makers. It would trace parallels with historical architecture that emphasizes association and symbolism, such as Romanticism, eclecticism, Mannerism, and the iconographic aspects of Gothic architecture, and tie these into the sign styles of Las Vegas.

In the seventeenth century, Rubens created a painting "factory" wherein different workers specialized in drapery, foliage, or nudes. In Las Vegas there is just such a sign "factory," the Young Electric Sign Company. Someone should talk to and observe and document each of the departments in YESCO; find out the backgrounds of the designers; watch the whole design process.

Is there a private vocabulary for sign designers such as that existing in architecture? How is the contradiction between form and function resolved in sign design? Carefully photograph the sign models.

How do people actually use Route 91, the median strips, the entrance ways to casinos, the parking lots, and the pedestrian access? How do they react to signs?

REPORT ON A SURVEY OF
DRIVERS ENTERING HOTEL
DRIVEWAYS

1. Most drivers took the first entrance available to them after becoming aware of the limits of the property of the place they desired to go to.

2. Most people disregarded the sign and planned internal workings of the parking lot as determined by the designer. Note the Circus Circus Casino sign.

3. The location of the signs and the other parking lot furniture seemed to have little influence on the use of the lot.

4. The *apparent* property line is a controlling element in the way people see the parking lot.

5. Visual elements, such as the fountains at Caesars Palace and Circus Circus, control the drivers more powerfully than any of the other directional signs. (John Kranz and Tony Zunino)

§ INCLUSION AND THE
DIFFICULT ORDER

"Modern systems! Yes, indeed! To approach everything in a strictly methodical manner and not to waver a hair's breadth from preconceived patterns, until genius has been strangled to death and *joie de vivre* stifled by the system—that is the sign of our time."
—Camillo Sitte[5]

"It is fruitless, however, to search for some dramatic key element or king pin which, if made clear, will clarify all. No single element in a city is, in truth, the king pin. The mixture is the king pin, and its mutual support is the order."
—Jane Jacobs[6]

"The key word is: Proportion. No matter what you may call it— beauty, eye appeal, good taste, or architectural compatibility, limiting the *size* of electrical advertising displays does not ensure any of these. Proper proportions —the relationship of graphic ele-

5. Camillo Sitte, *City Planning According to Artistic Principles*, translated by George R. Collins and Christiane Crasemann Collins (New York: Random House, 1965), p. 91.

6. Jane Jacobs, *The Death and Life of Great American Cities* (New York: Vintage Books, 1961), p. 376.

ments to each other—are necessary to good design, whether it
be a matter of clothing, art, architecture, or an electrical sign.
Relative size, not over-all size,
is the factor in determining
guidelines which will satisfac-
torily influence attractive appearance."
—California Electric Sign Association[7]
Should a gas station on the
Strip be required to blend with
(that is, look like) the casinos?

How can a design intention be
differentiated graphically from
one possible design among many
that might stem from a design
control?

Computer-video urban simulation systems suggest possibilities
for controls to be tried out
through the simulation of environments. Imaginatively used,
this could make for looser yet
more efficient controls.

CONTROLS AND BEAUTIFICATION
The Las Vegas Strip "just
grew," and perhaps its initiators
built it outside the city limits in
order to escape controls. But today there are the usual building
and zoning controls and a "Strip
Beautification Committee" as
well (Fig. 69). There is no good
record of commissions on aesthetics producing good architecture.[8] (Haussmann was not a

7. "Guideline Standards for On Prem-
ise Signs," prepared specifically for
Community Planning Authorities by
California Electric Sign Association,
Los Angeles, Calif. (1967), p. 14.

8. See Appendix.

commission but a one-man control system. His power and its results are dubiously desirable and
certainly unattainable today.)
Commissions produce mediocrity
and a deadened urb. What will
happen to the Strip when the
tastemakers take over?

SIGN CONTROL
The basic premises of three
major parties are as follows:
Aesthetician: "Urban environment as medium of communication. . . . Signs should enhance
and clarify this communication."
Sign Industry: "Signs are good,
they're good for business, that
makes 'um good for H'america
too."
Legal Statutes: "If you'll just
perform these minimal requirements we can collect a fee for
the city and you gentlemen can
continue your sender-message-
receiver responses."
(Charles Korn)

§ IMAGE OF LAS VEGAS:
INCLUSION AND ALLUSION
IN ARCHITECTURE (FIGS. 71,
72)

An image employed by a designer should be something very
evocative, something that does
not limit by being too defined
and too concrete, yet helps the
designer think of the city in
physical terms. Laughing or cry-
ing faces or people sitting at
gambling machines are not
enough. What is an urban designer's image, or set of images, for

the Strip and the big low spaces of the casinos? What techniques—movie, graphic, or other—should be used to depict them?

In the eighteenth and nineteenth centuries an integral part of an architect's education consisted of sketching Roman ruins. If the eighteenth-century architect discovered his design gestalt by means of the Grand Tour and a sketch pad, we as twentieth-century architects will have to find our own "sketch pad" for Las Vegas.

We feel that we should construct our visual image of Las Vegas by means of a collage made from Las Vegas artifacts of many types and sizes, from YESCO signs to the Caesars Palace daily calendar. To construct this collage, you should collect images, verbal slogans, and objects. Bear in mind that, however diverse the pieces, they must be juxtaposed in a meaningful way, for example, as are Rome and Las Vegas in this study. Document the American piazza versus the Roman, and Nolli's Rome versus the Strip.

PART II

UGLY AND ORDINARY ARCHITECTURE, OR THE DECORATED SHED

SOME DEFINITIONS USING
THE COMPARATIVE METHOD

"Not innovating willfulness but reverence for the archetype."
Herman Melville

"Incessant new beginnings lead to sterility."
Wallace Stevens

"I like boring things."
Andy Warhol

To make the case for a new but old direction in architecture, we shall use some perhaps indiscreet comparisons to show what we are for and what we are against and ultimately to justify our own architecture. When architects talk or write, they philosophize almost solely to justify their own work, and this apologia will be no different. Our argument depends on comparisons, because it is simple to the point of banality. It needs contrast to point it up. We shall use, somewhat undiplomatically, some of the works of leading architects today as contrast and context.

We shall emphasize image—image over process or form—in asserting that architecture depends in its perception and creation on past experience and emotional association and that these symbolic and representational elements may often be contradictory to the form, structure, and program with which they combine in the same building. We shall survey this contradiction in its two main manifestations:

1. Where the architectural systems of space, structure, and program are submerged and distorted by an overall symbolic form. This kind of building-becoming-sculpture we call the *duck* in honor of the duck-shaped drive-in, "The Long Island Duckling," illustrated in *God's Own Junkyard* by Peter Blake (Fig. 73).[1]

2. Where systems of space and structure are directly at the service of program, and ornament is applied independently of them. This we call the *decorated shed* (Fig. 74).

The duck is the special building that *is* a symbol; the decorated shed is the conventional shelter that *applies* symbols (Figs. 75, 76). We maintain that both kinds of architecture are valid—Chartres is a duck (although it is a decorated shed as well), and the Palazzo Farnese is a decorated shed—but we think that the duck is seldom relevant today, although it pervades Modern architecture.

We shall describe how we come by the automobile-oriented commer-

1. Peter Blake, *God's Own Junkyard: The Planned Deterioration of America's Landscape* (New York: Holt, Rinehart and Winston, 1964), p. 101. See also Denise Scott Brown and Robert Venturi, "On Ducks and Decoration," *Architecture Canada* (October 1968).

73. "Long Island Duckling" from *God's Own Junkyard*

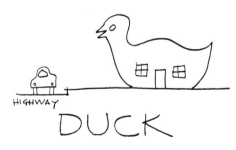

75. Duck

74. Road scene from *God's Own Junkyard*

76. Decorated shed

cial architecture of urban sprawl as our source for a civic and residential architecture of meaning, viable now, as the turn-of-the-century industrial vocabulary was viable for a Modern architecture of space and industrial technology 40 years ago. We shall show how the iconography, rather than the space and piazzas of historical architecture, forms the background for the study of association and symbolism in commercial art and strip architecture.

Finally we shall argue for the symbolism of the ugly and ordinary in architecture and for the particular significance of the decorated shed with a rhetorical front and conventional behind: for architecture as shelter with symbols on it.

THE DUCK AND THE DECORATED SHED

Let us elaborate on the decorated shed by comparing Paul Rudolph's Crawford Manor with our Guild House (in association with Cope and Lippincott; Figs. 77, 78). These two buildings are comparable in use, size, and date of construction: Both are high-rise apartments for the elderly, consisting of about 90 units, built in the mid-1960s. Their settings vary: Guild House, although freestanding, is a six-story imitation palazzo, analogous in structure and materials to the surrounding buildings and continuing, through its position and form, the street line of the Philadelphia gridiron plan it sits in. Crawford Manor, on the other hand, is unequivocally a soaring tower, unique in its Modern, Ville Radieuse world along New Haven's limited-access Oak Street Connector.

But it is the contrast in the *images* of these buildings in relation to their systems of construction that we want to emphasize. The system of construction and program of Guild House are ordinary and conventional and look it; the system of construction and program of Crawford Manor are ordinary and conventional but do not look it.

Let us interject here that we chose Crawford Manor for this comparison not because of any particular antagonism toward that building. It is, in fact, a skillful building by a skillful architect, and we could easily have chosen a much more extreme version of what we are criticizing. But in general we chose it because it can represent establishment architecture now (that is, it represents the great majority of what you see today in any architecture journal), and in particular because it corresponds in fundamental ways with Guild House. On the other hand, our choosing Guild House for comparison involves a disadvantage, because that building is now five years old, and some of our later work can more explicitly and vividly convey our current ideas. Last, please do not criticize us for primarily analyzing image: We are doing so simply because image is pertinent to our argument, not because we wish to deny an interest in or the importance of process, program, and structure or, indeed, social issues in architecture or in these two buildings. Along with most architects, we probably spend 90 percent of our design time on these other important subjects and less than 10 percent on the questions we are addressing here; they are merely not the direct subject of this inquiry.

To continue our comparisons, the construction of Guild House is poured-in-place concrete plate with curtain walls, pierced by double-hung windows and enclosing the interior space to make rooms. The material is common brick—darker than usual to match the smog-smudged brick of the neighborhood. The mechanical systems of Guild House are nowhere manifest in the outside forms. The typical floor plan contains a 1920s-apartment-house variety of units to accommodate particular needs, views, and exposures; this distorts the efficient grid of columns (Fig. 80). The structure of Crawford Manor, which is poured-in-place concrete with concrete block faced with a striated pattern, is likewise a conventional frame supporting laid-up masonry walls (Fig. 79). But it does not look it. It looks more advanced technologically and more progressive spatially. It looks as if its supports are spatial, perhaps mechanical-harboring shafts made of a continuous plastic material reminiscent of *béton brut* with the striated marks of violently heroic construction process embossed in their form. They articulate the flowing interior space, their structural purity never punctured by holes for windows or distorted by exceptions in the plan. Interior light is "modulated" by the voids between the structure and the "floating" cantilevered balconies (Fig. 81).

The architectural elements for supplying exterior light in Guild House are frankly windows. We relied on the conventional method of doing windows in a building, and we by no means thought through from the beginning the subject of exterior light modulation but started where someone else had left off before us. The windows look familiar; they *look like*, as well as *are*, windows, and in this respect their use is explicitly symbolic. But like all effective symbolic images, they are intended to look familiar and unfamiliar. They are the conventional element used slightly unconventionally. Like the subject matter of Pop Art, they are commonplace elements made uncommon through distortion in shape (slight), change in scale (they are much bigger than normal double-hung windows), and change in context (double-hung windows in a perhaps high-fashion building, Fig. 82).

DECORATION ON THE SHED

Guild House has ornament on it; Crawford Manor does not (Fig. 83). The ornament on Guild House is explicit. It both reinforces and contradicts the form of the building it adorns. And it is to some extent symbolic. The continuous stripe of white-glazed brick high on the facade, in combination with the plane of white-glazed brick below, divides the building into three uneven stories: basement, principal story, and attic. It contradicts the scale of the six real and equal floors on which it is imposed and suggests the proportions of a Renaissance palace. The central white panel also enhances the focus and scale of the entrance. It extends the ground floor to the top of the balcony of the second floor in the way, and for the same reasons, that the increased elaboration and scale around the door of a Renaissance palace or Gothic portal does. The exceptional and fat column in an otherwise flat wall surface increases the focus of the entrance, and the luxurious granite and glazed brick enhance the amenity there, as does the veined marble that developers apply at street level to make their apartment entrances more classy and rentable. At the same time, the column's position in the middle of the entrance diminishes its importance.

The arched window in Guild House is not structural. Unlike the more purely ornamental elements in this building, it reflects an interior function of the shed, that is, the common activities at the top. But the big common room itself is an exception to the system inside. On the front elevation, an arch sits above a central vertical stripe of balcony voids, whose base is the ornamental entrance. Arch, balconies, and base together unify the facade and, like a giant order (or classic jukebox front), undermine the six stories to increase the scale and monumentality of the front. In turn, the giant order is topped by a flourish, an unconnected, symmetrical television antenna in gold anodized aluminum, which is both an imitation of an abstract Lippold sculpture and symbol for the elderly. An open-armed, polychromatic, plaster madonna in this position would have been more imageful but unsuitable for a Quaker institution that eschews all outward symbols—as do Crawford Manor and most orthodox Modern architecture, which reject ornament and association in the perception of forms.

EXPLICIT AND IMPLICIT ASSOCIATIONS

Adornments of representational sculpture on the roof, or a prettily shaped window, or wittiness or rhetoric of any kind are unthinkable for Crawford Manor. Nor would it sport appliqués of expensive material on a column or white stripes and wainscoting copied from Renaissance compositions. For instance, Crawford Manor's cantilevered balconies are "structurally integrated"; they are parapeted with the overall structural material and devoid of ornament. Balconies at Guild House are not structural exercises, and the railings are adornments as well as recollections at a bigger scale of conventional patterns in stamped metal (Fig. 84).

Guild House symbolism involves ornament and is more or less dependent on explicit associations; it looks like what it is not only because of what it is but also because of what it reminds you of. But the architectural elements of Crawford Manor abound in associations of another, less explicit, kind. Implicit in the pure architectural forms of Crawford Manor is a symbolism different from the appliqué ornament of Guild House with its explicit, almost heraldic, associations. The implicit symbolism of Crawford Manor we read into the undecorated physiognomy of the building through associations and past experience; it provides layers of meaning beyond the "abstract expressionist" messages derived from the inherent physiognomic characteristics of the forms—their size, texture, color, and so forth. These meanings come from our knowledge of technology, from the work and writings of the Modern form givers, from the vocabulary of industrial architecture, and from other sources. For instance, the vertical shafts of Crawford Manor connote structural piers (they are not structural), made of rusticated "reinforced concrete" (with mortar joints), harboring servant spaces and mechanical systems (actually kitchens), terminating in the silhouettes of exhaust systems (suitable to industrial laboratories), articulating light-modulating voids (instead of framing windows), articulating flowing space (confined to efficiency apartments but augmented by very ubiquitous balconies that themselves suggest apartment dwelling), and articulating program functions that protrude sensitively (or expressionistically) from the edges of the plan.

HEROIC AND ORIGINAL, OR UGLY AND ORDINARY

The content of Crawford Manor's implicit symbolism is what we call "heroic and original." Although the substance is conventional and ordinary, the image is heroic and original. The content of the explicit symbolism of Guild House is what we call "ugly and ordinary." The technologically unadvanced brick, the old-fashioned, double-hung windows, the pretty materials around the entrance, and the ugly antenna not hidden behind the parapet in the accepted fashion, all are distinctly conventional in image as well as substance or, rather, ugly and ordinary. (The inevitable plastic flowers at home in these windows are, rather, *pretty* and ordinary; they do not make this architecture look silly as they would, we think, the heroic and original windows of Crawford Manor, Fig. 85.)

But in Guild House, the symbolism of the ordinary goes further than this. The pretensions of the "giant order" on the front, the symmetrical, palazzolike composition with its three monumental stories (as well as its six real stories), topped by a piece of sculpture—or almost sculpture—suggest something of the heroic and original. It is true that in this

77. Crawford Manor, New Haven, 1962-1966; Paul Rudolph

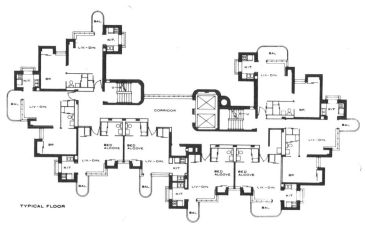

TYPICAL FLOOR

79. Crawford Manor, typical plan

78. Guild House, Friends' Housing for the Elderly, Philadelphia, 1960-1963;
Venturi and Rauch, Cope and Lippincott, Associates

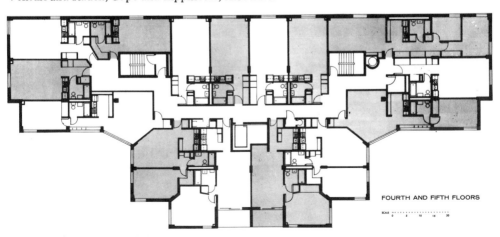

FOURTH AND FIFTH FLOORS

SCALE

80. Guild House, typical plan

81. Crawford Manor (detail)

82. Guild House, windows

83. Guild House, central panel

84. Guild House, balcony

85. Guild House, detail of window

86. Guild House, sign

case the heroic and original facade is somewhat ironical, but it is this juxtaposition of contrasting symbols—the appliqué of one order of symbols on another—that constitutes for us the decorated shed. This is what makes Guild House an architect's decorated shed—not architecture without architects.

The purest decorated shed would be some form of conventional systems-building shelter that corresponds closely to the space, structure, and program requirements of the architecture, and upon which is laid a contrasting—and, if in the nature of the circumstances, contradictory—decoration. In Guild House the ornamental-symbolic elements are more or less literally appliqué: The planes and stripes of white brick are appliqué; the street facade through its disengagement at the top corners implies its separation from the bulk of the shed at the front. (This quality also implies continuity, and therefore unity, with the street line of facades of the other older, nonfreestanding buildings on each side.) The symbolism of the decoration happens to be ugly and ordinary with a dash of ironic heroic and original, and the shed is straight ugly and ordinary, though in its brick and windows it is symbolic too. Although there is ample historical precedent for the decorated shed, present-day roadside commercial architecture—the $10,000 stand with the $100,000 sign—was the immediate prototype of our decorated shed. And it is in the sign of Guild House that the purest manifestation of the decorated shed and the most vivid contrast with Crawford Manor lies.

ORNAMENT: SIGNS AND SYMBOLS, DENOTATION AND CONNOTATION, HERALDRY AND PHYSIOGNOMY, MEANING AND EXPRESSION

A sign on a building carries a denotative meaning in the explicit message of its letters and words. It contrasts with the connotative expression of the other, more architectural elements of the building. A big sign, like that over the entrance of Guild House, big enough to be read from passing cars on Spring Garden Street, is particularly ugly and ordinary in its explicit commercial associations (Fig. 86). It is significant that the sign for Crawford Manor is modest, tasteful, and not commercial. It is too small to be seen from fast-moving cars on the Oak Street Connector. But signs as explicit symbols, especially big, commercial-looking signs, are anathema in architecture such as Crawford Manor. Its identification comes, not through explicit, denotative communication, through literally spelling out "I am Guild House," but through the connotation implicit in the physiognomy of its pure architectural form, which is intended to express in some way housing for the elderly.

We have borrowed the simple literary distinctions between "denotative" and "connotative" meanings and applied them to the heraldic and physiognomic element in architecture. To clarify further, the sign saying GUILD HOUSE *denotes* meaning through its words; as such, it is the heraldic element *par excellence*. The character of the graphics, however, *connotes* institutional dignity, while, contradictorily, the size of the graphics *connotes* commercialism. The position of the sign perhaps also *connotes* entering. The white-glazed brick *denotes* decoration as a unique and rich appliqué on the normal red brick. Through the location of the white areas and stripes on the facade, we have tried *connotatively* to suggest floor levels associated with palaces and thereby palace-like scale and monumentality. The double-hung windows *denote* their function, but their grouping *connotes* domesticity and ordinary meanings.

Denotation indicates specific meaning; connotation suggests general meanings. The same element can have both denotative and connotative meanings, and these may be mutually contradictory. Generally, to the extent that it is denotative in its meaning, an element depends on its heraldic characteristics; to the extent that it is connotative, an element depends on its physiognomic qualities. Modern architecture (and Crawford Manor as its exemplar) has tended to shun the heraldic and denotative in architecture and to exaggerate the physiognomic and connotative. Modern architecture uses expressive ornament and shuns explicit symbolic ornament.

In sum, we have analyzed Guild House and Crawford Manor in terms of content of the image and in terms of method used to achieve image. A comparative catalog of Guild House versus Crawford Manor in these terms is shown in Table 1.

IS BORING ARCHITECTURE INTERESTING?

For all its commonness, is Guild House boring? For all its dramatic balconies, is Crawford Manor interesting? Is it not, perhaps, the other way around? Our criticism of Crawford Manor and the buildings it stands for is not moralistic, nor is it concerned with so-called honesty in architecture or a lack of correspondence between substance and image *per se*; Crawford Manor *is* ugly and ordinary while *looking* heroic and original. We criticize Crawford Manor not for "dishonesty," but for irrelevance today. We shall try to show how, in both the method and content of its images, Crawford Manor, as well as the architecture it represents, has impoverished itself by rejecting denotative ornament and the rich tradition of iconography in historical architecture and by ignoring—or rather using unawares—the connotative expression it substituted for decoration. When it cast out eclecticism, Modern architecture submerged symbolism. Instead it promoted expressionism, concentrating on the expression of architectural elements themselves: on the

Table 1. Comparison of Guild House and Crawford Manor

Guild House	Crawford Manor
An architecture of meaning	An architecture of expression
Explicit "denotative" symbolism	Implicit "connotative" symbolism
Symbolic ornament	Expressive ornament
Applied ornament	Integral expressionism
Mixed media	Pure architecture
Decoration by the attaching of superficial elements	Unadmitted decoration by the articulation of integral elements
Symbolism	Abstraction
Representational art	"Abstract expressionism"
Evocative architecture	Innovative architecture
Societal messages	Architectural content
Propaganda	Architectural articulation
High *and* low art	High art
Evolutionary, using historical precedent	Revolutionary, progressive, anti-traditional
Conventional	Creative, unique, and original
Old words with new meanings	New words
Ordinary	Extraordinary
Expedient	Heroic
Pretty in front	Pretty (or at least unified) all around
Inconsistent	Consistent
Conventional technology	Advanced technology
Tendency toward urban sprawl	Tendency toward megastructure
Starts from client's value system	Tries to elevate client's value system and/or budget by reference to Art and Metaphysics
Looks cheap	Looks expensive
"Boring"	"Interesting"

expression of structure and function. It suggested, through the image of the building, reformist-progressive social and industrial aims that it could seldom achieve in reality. By limiting itself to strident articulations of the pure architectural elements of space, structure, and program, Modern architecture's expression has become a dry expressionism, empty and boring—and in the end irresponsible. Ironically, the Modern architecture of today, while rejecting explicit symbolism and frivolous appliqué ornament, has distorted the whole building into one big ornament. In substituting "articulation" for decoration, it has become a duck.

HISTORICAL AND OTHER PRECEDENTS: TOWARDS AN OLD ARCHITECTURE

HISTORICAL SYMBOLISM AND MODERN ARCHITECTURE

The forms of Modern architecture have been created by architects and analyzed by critics largely in terms of their perceptual qualities and at the expense of their symbolic meanings derived from association. To the extent that the Moderns recognize the systems of symbols that pervade our environment, they tend to refer to the debasement of our symbols. Although largely forgotten by Modern architects, the historical precedent for symbolism in architecture exists, and the complexities of iconography have continued to be a major part of the discipline of art history. Early Modern architects scorned recollection in architecture. They rejected eclecticism and style as elements of architecture as well as any historicism that minimized the revolutionary over the evolutionary character of their almost exclusively technology-based architecture. A second generation of Modern architects acknowledged only the "constituent facts" of history, as extracted by Sigfried Giedion,[2] who abstracted the historical building and its piazza as pure form and space in light. These architects' preoccupation with space as *the* architectural quality caused them to read the buildings as forms, the piazzas as space, and the graphics and sculpture as color, texture, and scale. The ensemble became an abstract expression in architecture in the decade of abstract expressionism in painting. The iconographic forms and trappings of medieval and Renaissance architecture were reduced to polychromatic texture at the service of space; the symbolic complexities and contradictions of Mannerist architecture were appreciated for their formal complexities and contradictions; Neoclassical architecture was liked, not for its Romantic use of association, but for its formal simplicity. Architects liked the *backs* of nineteenth century railroad stations—literally the sheds—and tolerated the fronts as irrelevant, if amusing, aberrations of historical eclecticism. The symbol systems developed by the commercial artists of Madison Avenue, which constitute the symbolic ambience of urban sprawl, they did not acknowledge.

In the 1950s and 1960s, these "Abstract Expressionists" of Modern architecture acknowledged one dimension of the hill town-piazza complex: its "pedestrian scale" and the "urban life" engendered by its architecture. This view of medieval urbanism encouraged the megastructural (or megasculptural?) fantasies—in this context hill towns with technological trimmings—and reinforced the antiautomobile bias of the Modern architect. But the competition of signs and symbols in the

2. Sigfried Giedion, *Space, Time and Architecture* (Cambridge, Mass.: Harvard University Press, 1944), Part I.

medieval city at various levels of perception and meaning in both building and piazza was lost on the space-oriented architect. Perhaps the
symbols, besides being foreign in content, were at a scale and a degree
of complexity too subtle for today's bruised sensibilities and impatient
pace. This explains, perhaps, the ironical fact that the return to iconography for some of us architects of that generation was via the sensibilities of the Pop artists of the early 1960s and via the duck and the decorated shed on Route 66: from Rome to Las Vegas, but also back again
from Las Vegas to Rome.

THE CATHEDRAL AS DUCK AND SHED

In iconographic terms, the cathedral is a decorated shed *and* a duck.
The Late Byzantine Metropole Cathedral in Athens is absurd as a piece
of architecture (Fig. 87). It is "out of scale": Its small size does not correspond to its complex form—that is, if form must be determined primarily by structure—because the space that the square room encloses
could be spanned without the interior supports and the complex roof
configuration of dome, drum, and vaults. However, it is not absurd as a
duck—as a domed Greek cross, evolved structurally from large buildings
in greater cities, but developed symbolically here to mean cathedral.
And this duck is itself decorated with an appliqué collage of *objets
trouvés*—bas-reliefs in masonry—more or less explicitly symbolic in content.

Amiens Cathedral is a billboard with a building behind it (Fig. 88).
Gothic cathedrals have been considered weak in that they did not
achieve an "organic unity" between front and side. But this disjunction
is a natural reflection of an inherent contradiction in a complex building that, toward the cathedral square, is a relatively two-dimensional
screen for propaganda and, in back, is a masonry systems building. This
is the reflection of a contradiction between image and function that the
decorated shed often accommodates. (The shed behind is also a duck
because its shape is that of a cross.)

The facades of the great cathedrals of the Ile de France are two-
dimensional planes at the scale of the whole; they were to evolve at the
top corners into towers to connect with the surrounding countryside.
But in detail these facades are buildings in themselves, simulating an
architecture of space in the strongly three-dimensional relief of their
sculpture. The niches for statues—as Sir John Summerson has pointed
out—are yet another level of architecture within architecture. But the
impact of the facade comes from the immensely complex meaning derived from the symbolism and explicit associations of the aedicules and
their statues and from their relative positions and sizes in the hierarchic
order of the kingdom of heaven on the facades. In this orchestration of

messages, connotation as practiced by Modern architects is scarcely important. The shape of the facade, in fact, disguises the silhouette of nave and aisles behind, and the doors and the rose windows are the barest reflections of the architectural complex inside.

SYMBOLIC EVOLUTION IN LAS VEGAS

Just as the architectural evolution of a typical Gothic cathedral may be traced over the decades through stylistic and symbolic changes, a similar evolution—rare in contemporary architecture—may also be followed in the commercial architecture of Las Vegas. However, in Las Vegas, this evolution is compressed into years rather than decades, reflecting the quicker tempo of our times, if not the less eternal message of commercial rather than religious propaganda. Evolution in Las Vegas is consistently toward more and bigger symbolism. The Golden Nugget casino on Fremont Street was an orthodox decorated shed with big signs in the 1950s—essentially Main Street commercial, ugly and ordinary (Fig. 89). However, by the 1960s it was all sign; there was hardly any building visible (Fig. 90). The quality of the "electrographics" was made more strident to match the crasser scale and more distracting context of the new decade and to keep up with the competition next door. The freestanding signs on the Strip, like the towers at San Gimignano, get bigger as well. They grow either through sequential replacements, as at the Flamingo, the Desert Inn, and the Tropicana, or through enlargement as with the Caesars Palace sign, where a freestanding, pedimented temple facade was extended laterally by one column with a statue on top—a feat never attempted, a problem never solved in the whole evolution of Classical architecture (Fig. 91).

THE RENAISSANCE AND THE DECORATED SHED

The iconography of Renaissance architecture is less overtly propagandistic than is that of medieval or Strip architecture, although its ornament, literally based on the Roman, Classical vocabulary, was to be an instrument for the rebirth of classical civilization. However, since most of this ornament depicts structure—it is ornament symbolic of structure—it is less independent of the shed it is attached to than ornament on medieval and Strip architecture (Fig. 92). The image of the structure and space reinforces rather than contradicts the substance of the structure and space. Pilasters represent modular sinews on the surface of the wall; quoins represent reinforcement at the ends of the wall; vertical moldings, protection at the edges of the wall; rustication, support at the bottom of the wall; drip cornices, protection from rain on the wall; horizontal moldings, the progressive stages in the depth of the wall; and a combination of many of these ornaments at the edge of a door symbolizes the importance of the door in the face of the wall. Although some of these elements are functional as well—for instance, the drips are, but the pilasters are not—all are explicitly symbolic, associating the glories of Rome with the refinements of building.

But Renaissance iconography is not all structural. The *stemma* above the door is a sign. The Baroque facades of Francesco Borromini, for instance, are rich with symbolism in bas-relief—religious, dynastic, and other. It is significant that Giedion, in his brilliant analysis of the facade of San Carlo alle Quattro Fontane, described the contrapuntal layerings, undulating rhythms, and subtle scales of the forms and surfaces as abstract elements in a composition in relation to the outside space of the street but without reference to the complex layering of symbolic meanings they contain.

The Italian palace is the decorated shed *par excellence*. For two centuries, from Florence to Rome, the plan of rooms *en suite* around a rectangular, arcaded *cortile* with an entrance penetration in the middle of a facade and a three-story elevation with occasional mezzanines was a constant base for a series of stylistic and compositional variations. The architectural scaffolding was the same for the Strozzi Palace with its three stories of diminishing rustication, for the Rucellai with its quasi-frame of three-ordered pilasters, for the Farnese with its quoined corners complementing the focus of the ornamental central bay and its resultant horizontal hierarchy, and for the Odescalchi with its monumental giant order imposing the image of one dominant story on three (Figs. 93, 94). The basis for the significant evaluation of the development of Italian civic architecture from the mid-fifteenth to the mid-seventeenth century lies in the decoration of a shed. Similar ornament adorns subsequent palazzi, commercial and *senza cortili*. The Carson Pirie Scott department store supports at the ground floor a cast-iron cladding of biological patterns in low relief with intricate scale appropriate for sustaining the customers' interest at eye level, while abruptly opposing, in the formal vocabulary above it, the ugly and ordinary symbolism of a conventional loft (Fig. 95). The conventional shed of a high-rise Howard Johnson motel is more Ville Radieuse slab than palazzo, but the explicit symbolism of its virtually pedimented doorway, a rigid frame in heraldic orange enamel, matches the Classical pediment with feudal crest over the entrance of a patrician palazzo, if we grant the change in scale and the jump in context from urban piazza to Pop sprawl (Fig. 96).

NINETEENTH-CENTURY ECLECTICISM

The stylistic eclecticism of the nineteenth century was essentially a symbolism of function, although sometimes a symbolism of nationalism

87. Metropole Cathedral, Athens

88. Amiens Cathedral, west front

89. Golden Nugget, Las Vegas, pre-1964

90. Golden Nugget, Las Vegas, post-1964

91. Caesars Palace, extended sign

92. Belvedere Court, Vatican

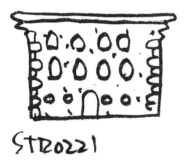

STROZZI

FARNESE

RVCELLAI

ODESCALCHI

93-94. Palazzo facades

95. Carson Pirie Scott department store, Chicago

96. Howard Johnson's Motor Lodge and Restaurant,
Charlottesville, Virginia

97. Eclectic bank

98. Eclectic church

99. Hamburger stand, Dallas, Texas

—Henri IV Renaissance in France, Tudor in England, for example. But quite consistently styles correspond to building types. Banks were Classical basilicas to suggest civic responsibility and tradition; commercial buildings looked like burghers' houses; universities copied Gothic rather than Classical colleges at Oxford and Cambridge to make symbols of "embattled learning," as George Howe put it, "tending the torch of humanism through the dark ages of economic determinism,"[3] and a choice between Perpendicular and Decorated for midcentury English churches reflected theological differences between the Oxford and Cambridge Movements. The hamburger-shaped hamburger stand is a current, more literal, attempt to express function via association but for commercial persuasion rather than theological refinement (Figs. 97-99).

Donald Drew Egbert,[4] in an analysis of midcentury submissions for the Prix de Rome at the Ecole des Beaux-Arts—home of the bad guys—called functionalism via association a symbolic manifestation of functionalism that preceded the substantive functionalism that was a basis for the Modern movement: Image preceded substance. Egbert also discussed the balance in the new nineteenth-century building types between expression of function via physiognomy and expression of function via style. For instance, the railroad station was recognizable by its cast-iron shed and big clock. These physiognomic symbols contrasted with the explicit heraldic signing of the Renaissance-eclectic waiting and station spaces up front. Sigfried Giedion called this artful contrast within the same building a gross contradiction—a nineteenth-century "split in feeling"—because he saw architecture as technology and space, excluding the element of symbolic meaning.

MODERN ORNAMENT

Modern architects began to make the back the front, symbolizing the configurations of the shed to create a vocabulary for their architecture but denying in theory what they were doing in practice. They said one thing and did another. Less may have been more, but the I-section on Mies van der Rohe's fire-resistant columns, for instance, is as complexly ornamental as the applied pilaster on the Renaissance pier or the incised shaft in the Gothic pier. (In fact, less was more work.) Acknowledged or not, Modern ornament has seldom been symbolic of anything nonarchitectural since the Bauhaus vanquished Art Deco and the decorative arts. More specifically, its content is consistently spatial and technological. Like the Renaissance vocabulary of the Classical orders, Mies's

3. George Howe, "Some Experiences and Observations of an Elderly Architect," *Perspecta 2, The Yale Architectural Journal*, New Haven (1954), p. 4.

4. Donald Drew Egbert, "Lectures in Modern Architecture" (unpublished), Princeton University, c. 1945.

structural ornament, although specifically contradictory to the structure it adorns, reinforces the architectural content of the building as a whole. If the Classical orders symbolized "rebirth of the Golden Age of Rome," modern I-beams represent "honest expression of modern technology as space"—or something like that. Note, however, it was "modern" technology of the Industrial Revolution that was symbolized by Mies, and this technology, not current electronic technology, is still the source for Modern architectural symbolism today.

ORNAMENT AND INTERIOR SPACE

Mies's I-section appliqués represent naked steel-frame construction, and they make the necessarily bulky, enclosed, fire-resistant frame underneath look thinner through their complex articulations. Mies used ornamental marble in his early interiors to define space. The marble and marblelike panels in the Barcelona Pavilion, the House with Three Courts, and other buildings of that period are less symbolic than the later exterior pilasters, although the lush veneering of the marble and its reputation for rarity connote richness (Fig. 100). Although these "floating" panels can now almost be mistaken for abstract expressionist easel paintings of the 1950s, their purpose was to articulate Flowing Space by directing it within a linear steel frame. Ornament is the servant of Space.

The Kolbe sculpture in this pavilion may have certain symbolic associations, but it too is there primarily to punctuate and direct space; it points up through contrast the machine aesthetic forms around it. A later generation of Modern architects has made these configurations of directional panels and punctuating sculpture the accepted technique for exhibition and museum display, giving the display elements an informational as well as a space-directing role. Mies's elements were symbolic rather than informational; they contrasted the natural with the machined, demonstrating what Modern architecture was by setting it against what it was not. Neither Mies nor his followers used the forms symbolically to convey other-than-architectural meaning. Social realism in a Mies pavilion would be as unthinkable as a WPA mural in the Petit Trianon (except that the flat roof itself was a symbol of socialism in the 1920s).

In the Renaissance interior too, ornament is used along with plenty of light to direct and punctuate space. But here in contrast with the Mies interiors, it is the constructional elements that are ornamental—the frames, moldings, pilasters, and architraves that reinforce the forms and identify enclosed space—while the surfaces are the neutral context. Inside the Mannerist Casino Pio V, however, pilasters, niches, architraves, and cornices obscure the nature of the space or, rather, make the distinction between wall and vault ambiguous, because these elements, traditionally identified with walls, extend over the vault's surface (Fig. 101).

In the chapel of the Byzantine Martorama in Sicily there is no question of architectural clarification or of Mannerist ambiguity (Fig. 102). Instead, representation smothers space, its patterns camouflaging the forms it adorns. The ornamental patterns are almost independent of, and at times contradictory to, walls, piers, soffits, vaults, and dome. These forms are rounded at their edges to accommodate continuous mosaic surfaces, and the gold mosaic background further softens the geometry, while in the obscure light that occasionally highlights significant symbols, space disintegrates into an amorphous glow. The gilded rocaille in the Amalienburg pavilion at Nymphenburg does the same thing with bas-relief (Fig. 103). Motival bas-relief, splattered like spinach over walls and furniture, hardware and sconces; reflected by mirrors and crystal fixtures; enhanced by generous light yet obscured by indeterminate curves in plan and section, disintegrates space into an amorphous glitter. Significantly, the Rococo ornament is hardly symbolic and not at all propagandistic. It obscures space, but the ornament is still architectural; in the Byzantine church, propagandistic symbolism overwhelms architecture.

THE LAS VEGAS STRIP

The Las Vegas Strip at night, like the Martorama interior, is symbolic images in dark, amorphous space; but, like the Amalienburg, it glitters rather than glows (Fig. 104). Any sense of enclosure or direction comes from lighted signs rather than forms reflected in light (Fig. 105). The source of light in the Strip is direct; the signs themselves are the source. They do not reflect light from external, sometimes hidden, sources as is the case with most billboards and Modern architecture. The mechanical movement of neon lights is quicker than mosaic glitter, which depends on the passage of the sun and the pace of the observer; and the intensity of light on the Strip as well as the tempo of its movement is greater to accommodate the greater spaces, greater speeds, and greater impacts that our technology permits and our sensibilities respond to. Also, the tempo of our economy encourages that changeable and disposable environmental decoration known as advertising art. The messages are different now, but despite the differences the methods are the same, and architecture is no longer simply the "skillful, accurate, and magnificent play of masses seen in light."

The Strip by day is a different place, no longer Byzantine (Fig. 106). The forms of the buildings are visible but remain secondary to the signs in visual impact and symbolic content. The space of urban sprawl is not enclosed and directed as in traditional cities. Rather, it is open and indeterminate, identified by points in space and patterns on the ground; these are two-dimensional or sculptural symbols in space rather than buildings in space, complex configurations that are graphic or representational. Acting as symbols, the signs and buildings identify the space by their location and direction, and space is further defined and directed by utility poles and street and parking patterns. In residential sprawl the orientation of houses toward the street, their stylistic treatment as decorated sheds, and their landscaping and lawn fixtures—wagon wheels, mailboxes on erect chains, colonial lamps, and segments of split-rail fence—substitute for the signs of commercial sprawl as the definers of space (Figs. 107, 108).

Like the complex architectural accumulations of the Roman Forum, the Strip by day reads as chaos if you perceive only its forms and exclude its symbolic content. The Forum, like the Strip, was a landscape of symbols with layers of meaning evident in the location of roads and buildings, buildings representing earlier buildings, and the sculpture piled all over. Formally the Forum was an awful mess; symbolically it was a rich mix.

The series of triumphal arches in Rome is a prototype of the billboard (*mutatis mutandis* for scale, speed, and content). The architectural ornament, including pilasters, pediments, and coffers, is a kind of bas-relief that makes only a gesture toward architectural form. It is as symbolic as the bas-reliefs of processions and the inscriptions that compete for the surface (Fig. 109). Along with their function as billboards carrying messages, the triumphal arches in the Roman Forum were spatial markers channeling processional paths within a complex urban landscape. On Route 66 the billboards, set in series at a constant angle toward the oncoming traffic, with a standard distance between themselves and from the roadside, perform a similar formal-spatial function. Often the brightest, cleanest, and best-maintained elements in industrial sprawl, the billboards both cover and beautify that landscape. Like the configurations of sepulchral monuments along the Via Appia (again *mutatis mutandis* for scale), they mark the way through the vast spaces *beyond* urban sprawl. But these spatial characteristics of form, position, and orientation are secondary to their symbolic function. Along the highway, advertising Tanya via graphics and anatomy, like advertising the victories of Constantine via inscriptions and bas-reliefs, is more important than identifying the space (Fig. 110).

URBAN SPRAWL AND THE MEGASTRUCTURE

The urban manifestations of ugly and ordinary architecture and the decorated shed are closer to urban sprawl than to the megastructure

Table 2. Comparison of Urban Sprawl with Megastructure

Urban Sprawl	Megastructure
Ugly and ordinary	Heroic and original
Depends on explicit symbolism	Rejects explicit symbolism
Symbols in space	Forms in space
Image	Form
Mixed media	Pure architecture
Big signs designed by commercial artists	Little signs (and only if absolutely necessary) designed by "graphic artists"
Auto environment	Post- and pre-auto environment
Cars	Public transportation
Takes the parking lot seriously and pastiches the pedestrian	"Straight" architecture with serious but egocentric aims for the pedestrian; it irresponsibly ignores or tries to "piazzafy" the parking lot
Disneyland	Piazzas
Promoted by sales staff	Promoted by experts
Feasible and being built	Technologically feasible perhaps, but socially and economically unfeasible
Popular life-style	"Correct" life-style
Historical styles	Modern style
Uses typological models	Uses original creations
Process city	Instant city
Broadacre City	Ville Radieuse
Looks awful	Makes a nice model
Architects don't like	Architects like
20th-century communication technology	19th-century industrial vision
Social realism	Science fiction
Expedience	Technological indulgence
Expedient	Visionary
Ambiguous urban image	Traditional urban image
Vital mess	"Total Design" (and design review boards)
Building for markets	Building for Man
This year's problems	The old architectural revolution
Heterogeneous images	The image of the middle-class intelligentsia
The difficult image	The easy image
The difficult whole	The easy whole

(Figs. 111, 112). We have explained how, for us, commercial vernacular architecture was a vivid initial source for symbolism in architecture. We have described in the Las Vegas study the victory of symbols-in-space over forms-in-space in the brutal automobile landscape of great distances and high speed, where the subtleties of pure architectural space can no longer be savored. But the symbolism of urban sprawl lies also in its residential architecture, not only in the strident, roadside communications of the commercial strip (decorated shed or duck). Although the ranch house, split level or otherwise, conforms in its spatial configuration to several set patterns, it is appliquéd with varied though conforming ornament, evoking combinations of Colonial, New Orleans, Regency, Western, French Provincial, Modern, and other styles. Garden apartments—especially those of the Southwest—equally are decorated sheds whose pedestrian courts, like those of motels, are separate from, but close to, the automobile. A comparison of urban sprawl with the megastructure is made in Table 2.

Sprawl City's image (Fig. 113) is a result of process. In this respect it follows the canons of Modern architecture that require form to result from function, structure, and construction methods, that is, from the processes of its making. But for our time the megastructure (Fig. 114) is a distortion of normal city building process for the sake *inter alia* of image. Modern architects contradict themselves when they support functionalism *and* the megastructure. They do not recognize the image of the process city when they see it on the Strip, because it is both too familiar and too different from what they have been trained to accept.

100. House with Three Courts; perspective of bedroom wing; Mies van der Rohe

101. Casino Pio V, Rome

102. Martorama, Palermo

103. Amalienburg Pavilion, Nymphenburg

104. Fremont Street, Las Vegas

105. Las Vegas Strip at night

106. Las Vegas Strip by day

107. Suburban residential sprawl

108. Suburban mailbox

109. Arch of Constantine, Rome

110. Tanya billboard, Las Vegas

111. Las Vegas Strip

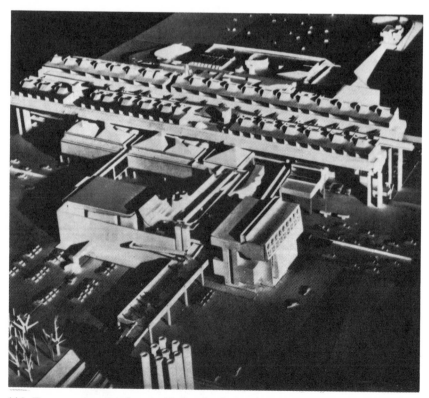

112. Town center, Cumbernauld, Scotland; Cumbernauld Development
Corporation

113. Residential strip

114. Habitat, Expo '67; Moshe Safdie

THEORY OF UGLY AND
ORDINARY AND RELATED
AND CONTRARY THEORIES

ORIGINS AND FURTHER DEFINITION OF UGLY
AND ORDINARY

Let us describe our own experience as architects to explain how we came to ugly and ordinary architecture. After the appearance of *Complexity and Contradiction in Architecture*,[5] we began to realize that few of our firm's buildings were complex and contradictory, at least not in their purely architectural qualities of space and structure as opposed to their symbolic content. We had failed to fit into our buildings double-functioning or vestigial elements, circumstantial distortions, expedient devices, eventful exceptions, exceptional diagonals, things in things, crowded or contained intricacies, linings or layerings, residual spaces, redundant spaces, ambiguities, inflections, dualities, difficult wholes, or the phenomena of both-and. There was little in our work of inclusion, inconsistency, compromise, accommodation, adaptation, superadjacency, equivalence, multiple focus, juxtaposition, or good *and* bad space.

Most of the complexities and contradictions we relished thinking about we did not use, because we did not have the opportunity. Venturi and Rauch did not get big commissions whose programs and settings justified complex and contradictory forms, and as artists we could not impose on our work inapplicable ideas that we liked as critics. A building should not be a vehicle for an architect's ideas, etc. Also our budgets were low, and we did not want to design a building twice— once to fit some heroic idea of its importance to society and the world of art and, after the bids came in, a second time to reflect the client's and society's restricted idea of our architecture's value. Whether society was right or wrong was not for us at that moment to argue. Therefore our Brighton Beach Housing entry did not turn out a megastructure for living in or our Fire Station in Columbus, Indiana, a personalized essay in civic monumentality for a pedestrian piazza by the side of the highway. They turned out "ugly and ordinary," as two such divergent critics as Philip Johnson and Gordon Bunshaft have described our work. "Ugly" or "beautiful" is perhaps a question of semantics in this context, but these two architects did catch the spirit, in a way.

Architecture may be ordinary—or rather, conventional—in two ways: in how it is constructed or in how it is seen, that is, in its process or in its symbolism. To construct conventionally is to use ordinary materials and engineering, accepting the present and usual organization of the

5. Robert Venturi, *Complexity and Contradiction in Architecture* (New York: The Museum of Modern Art and Graham Foundation, 1966).

building industry and its financial structure and hoping to ensure fast, sound, and economical construction. This is good in the short run, and the short run is what our clients have largely retained us architects for. Architectural theories of the short run tend toward the idealization and generalization of expediency. Architecture for the long run requires creation, rather than adaptation, and response to advanced technology and sophisticated organization. It depends on sound research that may perhaps be promoted in the architect's office but should be financed outside it, because the client's fee is not adequate for and not intended for that purpose. Although architects have not wished to recognize it, most architectural problems are of the expedient type, and the more architects become involved in social problems, the more this is true. In general the world cannot wait for the architect to build his or her utopia, and in the main the architect's concern should belong not with what ought to be but with what is—and with how to help improve it now. This is a humbler role for architects than the Modern movement has wanted to accept; however, it is artistically a more promising one.

UGLY AND ORDINARY AS SYMBOL AND STYLE

Artistically, the use of conventional elements in ordinary architecture —be they dumb doorknobs or the familiar forms of existing construction systems—evokes associations from past experience. Such elements may be carefully chosen or thoughtfully adapted from existing vocabularies or standard catalogs rather than uniquely created via original data and artistic intuition. To design a window, for instance, you start not only with the abstract function of modulating light rays and breezes to serve interior space but with the image of window—of all the windows you know plus others you find out about. This approach is symbolically and functionally conventional, but it promotes an architecture of meaning, broader and richer if less dramatic than the architecture of expression.

We have shown how heroic and original (H&O) architecture derives dramatic expression from the connotative meanings of its "original" elements: It gives off abstract meanings—or rather, expressions—recognizable in the physiognomic character of the architectural elements. Ugly and ordinary (U&O) architecture, on the other hand, includes denotative meanings as well, derived from its familiar elements; that is, it suggests more or less concrete meanings via association and past experience. The "brutalism" of an H&O fire station comes from its rough texture; its civic monumentality comes from its big scale; the expression of structure and program and "truth to materials" comes from the particular articulations of its forms. Its total image derives from these purely architectural qualities transmitted through abstract forms, tex-

tures, and colors, carefully composed (Fig. 115). The total image of our
U&O fire house—an image implying civic character as well as specific
use—comes from the conventions of roadside architecture that it follows; from the decorated false facade, from the banality through famil-
iarity of the standard aluminum sash and roll-up doors, and from the
flagpole in front—not to mention the conspicuous sign that identifies it
through spelling, the most denotative of symbols: FIRE STATION NO. 4
(Fig. 116). These elements act as symbols as well as expressive architectural abstractions. They are not merely ordinary but represent ordinari-
ness symbolically and stylistically; they are enriching as well, because
they add a layer of literary meaning.

Richness can come from conventional architecture. For 300 years
European architecture was variations on a Classical norm—a rich confor-
mity. But it can also come through an adjusting of the scale or context
of familiar and conventional elements to produce unusual meanings.
Pop artists used unusual juxtapositions of everyday objects in tense and
vivid plays between old and new associations to flout the everyday in-
terdependence of context and meaning, giving us a new interpretation
of twentieth-century cultural artifacts. The familiar that is a little off
has a strange and revealing power.

The double-hung window in Guild House is familiar in form but un-
usually large in size and horizontal in proportion, like the big, distorted
Campbell Soup can in Andy Warhol's painting. This typical window is
also juxtaposed with a smaller window of the same form and proportion. The exact location of the bigger window on a parallel plane behind the smaller window tends to disturb the habitual perception of distance through perspective; the resultant symbolic and optical tensions
are, we maintain, a means of making boring architecture interesting—a
more valid means than the irrelevant articulations of today's strident
but boring minimegastructures (Fig. 117).

AGAINST DUCKS, OR UGLY AND ORDINARY OVER HEROIC AND ORIGINAL, OR THINK LITTLE

We should not emphasize the ironic richness of banality in today's
artistic context at the expense of discussing the appropriateness and in-
evitability of U&O architecture on a wider basis. Why do we uphold the
symbolism of the ordinary via the decorated shed over the symbolism
of the heroic via the sculptural duck? Because this is not the time and
ours is not the environment for heroic communication through pure
architecture. Each medium has its day, and the rhetorical environmental statements of our time—civic, commercial, or residential—will come
from media more purely symbolic, perhaps less static and more adapt-

able to the scale of our environment. The iconography and mixed media of roadside commercial architecture will point the way, if we will look.

Housing for the elderly on the Oak Street Connector, if it had to be a monument, would have been more economical, socially responsible, and amenable as a conventional apartment building, lost by the side of the expressway, with a big sign on top blinking, I AM A MONUMENT. Decoration is cheaper (Fig. 139).

THEORIES OF SYMBOLISM AND ASSOCIATION IN ARCHITECTURE

Basic to the argument for the decorated shed is the assumption that symbolism is essential in architecture and that the model from a previous time or from the existing city is part of the source material, and the replication[6] of elements is part of the design method of this architecture. That is, architecture that depends on association in its perception depends on association in its creation.

We have approached the justification of symbolism in architecture pragmatically, using concrete examples, rather than abstractly through the science of semiotic or through *a priori* theorizing.[7] However, other approaches have rendered similar results. Alan Colquhoun has written of architecture as part of a "system of communications within society" and describes the anthropological and psychological basis for the use of a typology of forms in design, suggesting that not only are we not "free from the forms of the past, and from the availability of these forms as typological models, but that, if we assume we are free, we have lost control over a very active sector of our imagination and of our power to communicate with others."[8]

Colquhoun describes the essentially "representational" quality of the artifacts of primitive culture and their relationships, and discusses the continuing anthropological basis for "iconic values" in the products of technology. The cosmological systems of primitive peoples were not "close to nature" but intellectual and artificial. Colquhoun illustrates

6. G. Hersey, "Replication Replicated," *Perspecta 10, The Yale Architectural Journal*, New Haven (1955), pp. 211-248.

7. These abstract approaches have recently been explored in a series of essays edited by Charles Jencks and George Baird, *Meaning in Architecture* (New York: George Braziller, 1969). We are indebted particularly to the formulations of Charles Jencks, George Baird, and Alan Colquhoun.

8. Alan Colquhoun, "Typology and Design Method," *Arena, Journal of the Architectural Association* (June 1967), pp. 11-14, republished in Charles Jencks and George Baird, *Meaning in Architecture.*

this point by quoting from Claude Lévi-Strauss's description of kinship systems:[9]

> "Certainly the biological family is present and persists in human society. But what gives to kinship its character as a social fact is not what it must conserve of nature; it is the essential step by which it separates itself from nature. A system of kinship does not consist of objective blood ties; it exists only in the consciousness of men; it is an arbitrary system of representations, not the spontaneous development of a situation of fact."

Colquhoun claims that there is a

> "parallel between such systems and the way modern man still approaches the world. And what was true of primitive man in all the ramifications of his practical and emotional life—namely the need to *represent* the phenomenal world in such a way that it becomes a coherent and logical system—persists in our own organizations, and more particularly in our attitude toward the man-made objects of our environment."[10]

The perceptual-psychological necessity for representation in art and architecture in Colquhoun's argument is based on E. H. Gombrich's book *Meditations on a Hobby Horse.* Gombrich rejects the belief born of Modern Expressionist theory that "shapes have physiognomic or expressive content which communicates itself to us directly."[11] He demonstrates, Colquhoun says, that

> "the arrangement of forms such as found in a painting by Kandinsky is in fact very low in content, unless we attribute to these forms some system of conventional meanings not inherent in the forms themselves. His thesis is that physiognomic forms are ambiguous, though not wholly without expressive value, and that they can only be interpreted within a particular cultural ambience."[12]

Gombrich illustrates this by reference to the supposed inherent affective qualities of color exemplified in traffic signals; and Colquhoun cites the recent adoption by the Chinese of the color red for go, indicating action and forward movement, and of green for stop, indicating inaction and caution—this easy reversal itself indicating the triumph of con-

9. Claude Lévi-Strauss, *Structural Anthropology* (New York: Basic Books, 1963).

10. Colquhoun, "Typology and Design Method," pp. 11-14.

11. E. H. Gombrich, *Meditations on a Hobby Horse and Other Essays on Art* (London: Phaidon Press; Greenwich, Conn.: New York Graphic Society, 1963), pp. 45-69.

12. Colquhoun, "Typology and Design Method," pp. 11-14.

vention over physiognomy in our understanding of the meaning of form.

Colquhoun argues against the proposition of Modern architecture that form should be the result of the application of physical or mathematical laws rather than of previous association or aesthetic ideologies. Not only are these laws themselves human constructs, but in the real world, even the world of advanced technology, they are not totally determining; there are areas of free choice. If "in a world of pure technology this area is invariably dealt with by adapting previous solutions," then even more will this be the case in architecture where laws and facts are still less capable of leading directly to form. He grants that systems of representation are not altogether independent of the facts of the objective world, and indeed "the modern movement in architecture was an attempt to modify the representational systems which had been inherited from the pre-industrial past, and which had no longer seemed operable within the context of a rapidly changing technology."[13]

The viewing of physical laws and empirical facts as the fundamental source of form in Modern architectural theory Colquhoun calls "biotechnical determinism":

"And it is from this theory that the current belief in the supreme importance of scientific methods of analysis and classification derives. The essence of the functional doctrine of the modern movement was not that beauty or order or meaning were unnecessary, but that it could no longer be found in the deliberate search for final form, and the path by which the artifact affected the observer aesthetically was seen as short-circuiting the process of formalization. Form was merely the result of a logical process by which the operational needs and the operational techniques were brought together. Ultimately these would fuse in a kind of biological extension of life, and function and technology would become totally transparent."[14]

The limitations inherent in this approach, even for technical engineering problems, were acknowledged—obliquely—in Modern theory. But they were to be overcome through the integrating magic of intuition and without reference to historical models. That form results from intention as well as deterministic process was acknowledged in the writings of Le Corbusier, Laszlo Moholy-Nagy, and other leaders of the Modern movement in their descriptions of the "intuition," "imagination," "inventiveness," and "free and innumerable plastic events" that regulate architectural design. What resulted, Colquhoun says, was a "tension of two apparently contradictory ideas—biological determinism on one hand, and free expression on the other," within the doctrine of the

13. Ibid.
14. Ibid.

Modern movement. Through excluding a body of traditional practice for the sake of "science," a vacuum was left that was filled ironically by a form of permissive expressionism: "What appears on the surface as a hard, rational discipline of design, turns out rather paradoxically to be a mystical belief in the intuitive process."[15]

FIRMNESS + COMMODITY ≠ DELIGHT: MODERN ARCHITECTURE AND THE INDUSTRIAL VERNACULAR

Vitruvius wrote, via Sir Henry Wootton, that architecture was Firmness and Commodity and Delight. Gropius (or perhaps only his followers) implied, via the bio-technical determinism just described, that Firmness and Commodity equal Delight; that structure plus program rather simply result in form; that beauty is a by-product; and that—to tamper with the equation in another way—the process of making architecture becomes the image of architecture. Louis Kahn in the 1950s said that the architect should be surprised by the appearance of his design (Fig. 118).

Presumed in these equations is that process and image are never contradictory and that Delight is a result of the clarity and harmony of these simple relationships, untinged, of course, by the beauty of symbolism and ornament or by the associations of preconceived form: Architecture is frozen process.

The historians of the Modern movement concentrated on the innovative engineering structures of the nineteenth and early twentieth centuries as prototypes for Modern architecture, but it is significant that the bridges of Maillart are not architecture, and the hangars of Freysinnet are hardly architecture. As engineering solutions, their programs are simple and without the inherent contradictions of architectural programs. To traverse a ravine directly, safely, and cheaply or to protect a big space from the rain without intervening supports is all that is required of these structures. The unavoidable symbolic content of even such simple, utilitarian constructions and the unavoidable use of what Colquhoun calls typologies were ignored by the theorists of the Modern movement. The not infrequent ornamentation of these forms was excused as a deviant architectural hangover, characteristic of the times. But the ornamentation of utilitarian superstructures is typical of all times. The defensive walls of the medieval city were topped with elaborately varied crenelations and studded with rhetorically ornamented gates. The applied decorations of the classic structures of the Industrial Revolution (we see them as more classic than innovative) are another manifestation of the decorated shed—for example, the elaborated gusset plates of the frame bridges, or the modified Corinthian capitals of the fluted cast-iron columns in loft buildings, or the eclectically stylish en-

15. Ibid.

trances and fanciful parapets of their fronts.

The decoration of the shed in nineteenth-century industrial architecture was often ignored by architects and theorists of the Modern movement through selective viewing of buildings or through contrived cropping of photographs. Even today as architects stress the complexity of these buildings (for instance, the complex massing and clerestoried roof lines of the mills of the English industrial Midlands) rather than their simplicity, their not infrequent ornament is still discounted.

Mies van der Rohe looked at only the backs of Albert Kahn's factories in the Midwest and developed his minimal vocabulary of steel I-sections framing industrial sash. The fronts of Kahn's sheds almost always contained administrative offices and, being early twentieth-century creations, were graciously Art Deco rather than historical eclectic (Figs. 119, 120). The plastic massing up front, characteristic of this style, grandly contradicted the skeletal behind.

INDUSTRIAL ICONOGRAPHY

More important than Mies's forgetting the decoration was his copying the shed, that is, his deriving associations from the body of the building rather than from its facade. The architecture of the Modern movement, during its early decades and through a number of its masters, developed a vocabulary of forms based on a variety of industrial models whose conventions and proportions were no less explicit than the Classical orders of the Renaissance. What Mies did with linear industrial buildings in the 1940s, Le Corbusier had done with plastic grain elevators in the 1920s, and Gropius had done with the Bauhaus in the 1930s, imitating his own earlier factory, the Faguswerk, of 1911. Their factorylike buildings were more than "influenced" by the industrial vernacular structures of the then recent past, in the sense that historians have described influences among artists and movements. Their buildings were explicitly adapted from these sources, and largely for their symbolic content, because industrial structures *represented*, for European architects, the brave new world of science and technology. The architects of the early Modern movement, in discarding the admittedly obsolete symbolism of historical eclecticism, substituted that of the industrial vernacular. To put it another way, as Romantics still, they achieved a new sensibility through evoking the remote in place—that is, the contemporary industrial quarter on the other side of the tracks, which they transferred to the civic areas of the city—rather than evoking, as did the earlier Romantics, the remote in time through the replication of stylistic ornament of the past. That is, the Moderns employed a design method based on typological models and developed an architectural iconography based on their interpretation of the progressive technology of the Industrial Revolution (Fig. 121).

Colquhoun refers to the "iconic power" attributed by "those in the field of design who were—and are—preaching pure technology and so-called objective design method . . . to the creations of technology, which they worship to a degree inconceivable in a scientist."[16] He also writes of "the power of all artifacts to become icons . . . whether or not they were specifically created for this purpose," and he cites nineteenth-century steamships and locomotives as examples of objects "made ostensibly with utilitarian purposes in mind" which "quickly become gestalt entities . . . imbued with aesthetic unity" and symbolic quality. These objects, along with the factories and grain elevators, became explicit typological models that, despite what architects said to the contrary, significantly influenced the method of Modern architectural design and served as sources for its symbolic meanings.

INDUSTRIAL STYLING AND THE CUBIST MODEL

Later critics referred to a "machine aesthetic," and others have accepted the term, but Le Corbusier among the Modern masters was unique in elaborately describing industrial prototypes for his architecture in *Vers une Architecture* (Fig. 122). However, even he claimed the steamship and the grain elevator for their forms rather than their associations, for their simple geometry rather than their industrial image. It is significant, on the other hand, that the buildings of Le Corbusier, illustrated in his book, physically resemble the steamships and the grain elevators but not the Parthenon or the furniture in Santa Maria in Cosmedin or Michelangelo's details for Saint Peter's, which are also illustrated for their simple geometric forms. The industrial prototypes became literal models for Modern architecture, while the historical-architectural prototypes were merely analogs selected for certain of their characteristics. To put it another way, the industrial buildings were symbolically correct; the historical buildings were not.

For the abstract geometrical formalism of Le Corbusier's architecture at this time, Cubism was the model. It was the second model, in part countering that of the nautical-industrial images, and it accounted for the hovering, stuccoed planes that enveloped the industrial sash and spiral stairs in the Villa Savoye. Although historians describe the relation between painting and architecture of this period as a harmonious diffusion of the *Zeitgeist*, it was more an adaptation of the language of painting to that of architecture. The systems of pure, simple forms, sometimes transparent, that penetrate flowing space were explicitly

16. Ibid.

associated with Cubism and fitted Le Corbusier's famous definition, of that time, of architecture as "the skillful, accurate and magnificent play of masses seen in light."

SYMBOLISM UNADMITTED

A contradiction between what was said and what was done was typical of early Modern architecture: Walter Gropius decried the term "International Style" but created an architectural style and spread a vocabulary of industrial forms that were quite removed from industrial processes. Adolf Loos condemned ornament yet applied beautiful patterns in his own designs and would have erected the most magnificent, if ironic, symbol in the history of skyscrapers if he had won the *Chicago Tribune* competition. The later work of Le Corbusier started a continuing tradition of unacknowledged symbolism, whose indigenous-vernacular forms, in varying manifestations, are still with us.

But it is the contradiction—or at least the lack of correspondence—between image and substance that confirms the role of symbolism and association in orthodox Modern architecture. As we have said, the symbolism of Modern architecture is usually technological and functional, but when these functional elements work symbolically, they usually do not work functionally, for example, Mies's symbolically exposed but substantively encased steel frame and Rudolph's *béton brut* in concrete block or his "mechanical" shafts used for an apartment house rather than a research lab. Some latter-day Modern architectural contradictions are the use of flowing space for private functions, glass walls for western exposures, industrial clerestories for suburban high schools, exposed ducts that collect dust and conduct sound, mass-produced systems for underdeveloped countries, and the impressions of wooden formwork in the concrete of high-labor-cost economies.

We catalog here the failures of these functional elements to function as structure, program, mechanical equipment, lighting, or industrial process, not to criticize them (although on functional grounds they should be criticized), but to demonstrate their symbolism. Nor are we interested in criticizing the functional-technological content of early Modern architectural symbolism. What we criticize is the symbolic content of current Modern architecture and the architect's refusal to acknowledge symbolism.

Modern architects have substituted one set of symbols (Cubist-industrial-process) for another (Romantic-historical-eclecticism) but without being aware of it. This has made for confusing and ironic contradictions that are still with us. The diversity of styles (not to mention the syntactical correctness and suave precision) of the architecture of the 1960s might challenge the versatility of a Victorian eclectic of the 1860s. The following models serve as sources for symbolic representation in our best buildings today: Cape Kennedy launching pads (Fig. 123); the industrial vernacular of the English Midlands (Fig. 124); Victorian greenhouses (Fig. 125); Futurist zoots (Fig. 126); Constructivist protomegastructures (Fig. 127); space frames (Fig. 128); Piranesian *carceri* (Fig. 129); plastic forms indigenous to the Mediterranean (Fig. 130); pedestrian scale, medieval-space Tuscan hill towns (Fig. 131); and the works of the form givers of the Heroic period (Fig. 132).

FROM LA TOURETTE TO NEIMAN-MARCUS

The stylistic evolution from La Tourette to Neiman-Marcus is a characteristic development of form-giver symbolism in late Modern architecture. Le Corbusier's tense manifestation of late genius, a monastery in a Burgundian field (Fig. 133), is itself a brilliant adaptation of a white plastic vernacular of the eastern Mediterranean. Its forms became an Art and Architecture Building on a street corner in New Haven (Fig. 134), a brick laboratory on the campus at Cornell (Fig. 135), and a *palazzo pubblico* in a piazza in Boston (Fig. 136). A latest version of this Burgundian cloister is a department store off the Westheimer strip in suburban Houston—a pure symbol of progressive gentility set in a sea of parking (Figs. 137, 138). Again, we do not criticize these replications of a classic masterpiece in a different place for a different use, although we suggest the replication would have been done better if it had been accepted philosophically and used wittily, as in the case of a Beaux-Arts department store designed after an Italian palazzo. This series of buildings from Burgundy to Texas illustrates the Modern architect's tendency to glorify originality through copying it.

SLAVISH FORMALISM AND ARTICULATED EXPRESSIONISM

Substituting nonfunctioning imitations of a deterministic process for preconceived form has resulted not only in confusion and irony but in a formalism that is the more slavish for being unadmitted. Those planners and architects who decry formalism in architecture are frequently rigid and arbitrary when the time comes for committing their projects to form. Urban designers, having learned the antiformalist pieties of the architectural profession and the critique of "physical bias" of the planning profession, are often caught in this dilemma. Once the "planning process" has been planned and the "guidelines for development" have been set, plans are filled in with hypothetical buildings to show "possible developments" using the fashionable shapes of the architectural leader fancied by the recent graduate who happens to be "on the design side" of the project in the office at that time, whether or not this leader's formal vocabulary would be more relevant to the problem than some other formal vocabulary.

The substitution of expression for representation through disdain for symbolism and ornament has resulted in an architecture where expression has become expressionism. Owing perhaps to the meager meanings available from abstract forms and unadorned functional elements, the characteristic forms of late Modern architecture are often overstated. Conversely, they are often understated in their context as with Latourette on the Westheimer strip. Louis Kahn once called exaggeration the architect's tool to create ornament. But exaggeration of structure and program (and, in the 1950s and 1960s, mechanical equipment, that is, ducts equal decoration) has become a substitute for ornament.

ARTICULATION AS ORNAMENT

To replace ornament and explicit symbolism, Modern architects indulge in distortion and overarticulation. Strident distortion at large scale and "sensitive" articulation at small scale result in an expressionism that is, to us, meaningless and irrelevant, an architectural soap opera in which to be progressive is to look outlandish. On the one hand, consider all those residential, civic, and institutional buildings whose thin complexities (stepped terraces; accordion sections, or plans, or elevations; cantilevered clerestories; diagonal zoots; textured striations and flying bridges or buttresses) almost parallel the strident distortions of a McDonald's hamburger stand but lack the commercial program and distracting setting that justify the stridency of Strip architecture. On the other hand, consider sensitively articulated structural frames and cantilevered bays that modulate a facade, define interior spaces, or reflect variations in the program. These busy bumps and subtle dents are put there for scale and rhythm and richness too, but they are as irrelevant and meaningless as the pilaster bas-relief on a Renaissance palace (which they resemble), because they are seen mostly in big spaces (often parking lots) and at high speeds.

Articulated architecture today is like a minuet in a discotheque, because even off the highway our sensibilities remain attuned to its bold scale and detail. Perhaps in the cacaphonic context of our real landscape we are impatient with any architectural detail at all. Furthermore, sensitive articulation is an expensive luxury best eliminated before the bids come in. The two-foot cantilever on the face of a building, put there to suit a sensitive nuance of the program discerned only by the architect, is a hangover from more stable times. Today programs can change during the course of construction. We cannot afford too-literal conjunctions between form and transient functions. In sum, while today's forms are too strident for their function in our environment, to-

115. Central Fire Station, New Haven, 1959-1962; Earl P. Carlin, Architect; Paul E. Pozzi, Peter Millard, Associates

116. Fire Station No. 4, Columbus, Indiana, 1965-1967; Venturi and Rauch

117. Guild House, windows

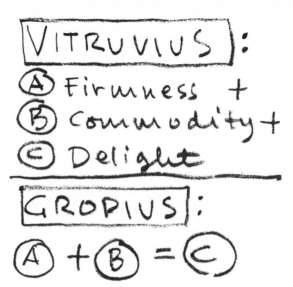

118. Vitruvius and Gropius

119. Plant for Lady Esther, Ltd., Clearing, Illinois; Albert Kahn

120. Plant for Lady Esther, Ltd.

121. Bauhaus, Dessau, Germany, 1925-1926; Walter Gropius

122. Grain elevator from Le Corbusier's
Towards a New Architecture

123. Cape Kennedy

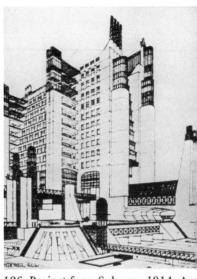

126. Project for a Subway, 1914; An Sant'Elia

124. St. Stephen's Maltings, Canterbury

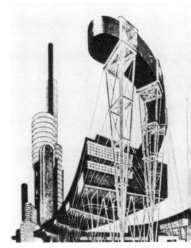

127. Russian Constructivist sketch industrial building from Tchernikov *101 Fantasies*

125. Palm House, Kew

128. Geodesic "Playdome"; Buckminster
Fuller

130. Procida, Italy

129. *Carceri*; Giovanni Battista Piranesi

131. Piazza Cavour, San Gimignano

132. High Court building, Chandigarh,
1951-1956; Le Corbusier

133. Monastery of La Tourette, Evreux, France, 1956-1960; Le Corbusier

134. Yale University Art and Architecture Building, New Haven, 1962-1963; Paul Rudolph

135. Cornell University Agronomy Building, Ithaca, New York, 1963-1968; Ulrich Franzen

136. City Hall, Boston, 1963; Kallman, McKinnell, and Knowles

137. Neiman-Marcus store, Houston, Texas; Hellmuth, Obata, and Kassabaum

138. Neiman-Marcus store

day's details are too sensitive for the timbre of our environment. However, at the opposite extreme, there is an individual need for intimacy and detail, unmet by Modern design but satisfied by the five-eighths scale reproductions in Disneyland, by the caricatures of human scale in the patios of garden apartments, and by the seven-eighths scale furnishings of the fancy interiors of Levittown model homes.

SPACE AS GOD

Perhaps the most tyrannical element in our architecture now is space. Space has been contrived by architects and deified by critics, filling the vacuum created by fugitive symbolism. If articulation has taken over from ornament in the architecture of abstract expressionism, space is what displaced symbolism. Our heroic and original symbols, from *carceri* to Cape Kennedy, feed our late Romantic egos and satisfy our lust for expressionistic, acrobatic space for a new age in architecture. It's space *and* light—light as an element for distorting space for further dramatization. The spatial replication today of the mills of the nineteenth-century industrial Midlands illustrates the irrelevance of these borrowings. The complex diagonal clerestories and sheer glass walls and roofs of early industrial architecture responded to the need for natural light and the availability of minimum artificial light for a 12-hour working day in a latitude where winter days are short and winters are long. On the other hand, the Manchester mill owner could depend on a cool climate in the summer, low heating standards in the winter and cheap and docile labor to put up with the conditions and repair the leaks. Today, however, most buildings need windows to look out of rather than glass walls for light, because our lighting standards are higher than can be satisfied through daylight alone, and areas of glass must be kept small and ceilings reasonably low to contain the air conditioning and meet the budget. Therefore our aesthetic impact should come from sources other than light, more symbolic and less spatial sources.

MEGASTRUCTURES AND DESIGN CONTROL

Recent Modern architecture has achieved formalism while rejecting form, promoted expressionism while ignoring ornament, and deified space while rejecting symbols. Confusions and ironies result from this unpleasantly complex and contradictory situation. Ironically we glorify originality through replication of the forms of Modern masters. There is little harm in this symbolic individualism except for its effect on the budget, but there *is* harm in imposing on the whole landscape heroic representations of the masters' unique creations. Such symbolic heroism lies behind the Modern proclivity for the megastructure and for total design. Architects who demand evidence of process in the forms of individual buildings reject it in the form of the city, where it is arguably more defensible. Total design is the opposite of the incremental city that grows through the decisions of many: total design conceives a messianic role for the architect as corrector of the mess of urban sprawl; it promotes a city dominated by pure architecture and maintained through "design review," and supports today's architecture of urban renewal and fine arts commissions. The Boston City Hall and its urban complex are the archetype of enlightened urban renewal. The profusion of symbolic forms, which recall the extravagances of the General Grant period, and the revival of the medieval piazza and its *palazzo pubblico* are in the end a bore. It is too architectural. A conventional loft would accommodate a bureaucracy better, perhaps with a blinking sign on top saying I AM A MONUMENT (Fig. 139).

However, no architecture is not the answer to too much architecture. The reaction of the antiarchitects of *Architectural Design* is perhaps as futile as the endless fondling of irrelevant subtleties at the other extreme in the other magazines, though it is possibly less harmful only because it seldom gets built, plugged in, or inflated. The world science futurist metaphysic, the megastructuralist mystique, and the look-Ma-no-buildings environmental suits and pods are a repetition of the mistakes of another generation. Their overdependence on a space-age, futurist, or science-fiction technology parallels the machine aestheticism of the 1920s and approaches its ultimate mannerism. They are, however, unlike the architecture of the 1920s, artistically a deadend and socially a cop-out.

The megastructure has been promoted by the elaborate journalism of groups such as Archigram who reject architecture but whose urban visions and mural-scale graphics go beyond the last, megalomaniac gasps of the late Beaux-Arts delineators. Unlike urban sprawl architecture, megastructures lend themselves to total design and to extremely beautiful models, significantly impressive in the boardrooms of cultural foundations or in the pages of *Time* magazine but unrelated to anything achievable or desirable in the present social or technical context. The occasionally witty exercises in Pop imagery of the megastructure visionaries are fine as an end in themselves, more literary than architectural in intent. They are a bore as architectural theory and ultimately, as well as immediately, unresponsive to the real and interesting problems now.

Meanwhile, every community and state is appointing its design review board to promote the architectural revolution of the last generation and corrupt its members through rule-by-man rather than rule-by-law procedures. "Total design" comes to mean "total control" as confident art commissioners who have learned what is right promote a deadening mediocrity by rejecting the "good" and the "bad" and the new they do not recognize, all of which, in combination and in the end, make the city. (See Appendix.)

MISPLACED TECHNOLOGICAL ZEAL

The old revolutionaries of the fine arts commissions and the new revolutionaries of the megastructures are, in our opinion, equally irrelevant, both socially and artistically. They also share the same tradition in architectural technology, taking the progressive, revolutionary, machine-aesthetic stance of the early Modern architects; part of being "heroic and original" is being advanced technologically. The discrepancies between substance and image in Modern architecture's technological *machismo* and the costliness of its frequently empty gestures emerged earlier than architects would admit. Methods of industrial production turned out to be largely inapplicable to the construction of buildings. Many elegant structural systems (space frames, for instance), although they were highly efficient in relating stress to material and economical for spanning large industrial structures, failed decisively to work within the program, space, and budget of the more prosaic and usual architectural commissions. As Philip Johnson said, you can't put a door in a geodesic dome.

Furthermore, many architects who concentrated on engineering forms ignored other aspects of the building industry, for example, financing, distribution, existing trades, and conventional materials and methods. These important facets, as the developers have known, are highly subject to the improving effects of technology, including managerial technology, and affect the final form and cost of architecture substantially more than does innovative constructional technology. Architects have contributed little to the crucial building needs of this country—especially in housing—partly because their predilections for advanced technology of the symbolic and visionary kind have impeded their effectiveness within the going systems of construction.

While focusing on their favorite form of technological voodooism over the last 40 years (that is, researching industrialized methods of prefabrication), architects have until recently ignored the mobile home industry. This industry, without the architects' help and using a traditional technology—essentially carpentry, which is then related to innovative methods of distribution—is now producing one-fifth of the annual output of housing in America. Architects should forget about being great technical innovators in housing construction and concentrate on adapting this new and useful technology to more broadly defined needs than it serves today and on developing a vivid mobile home symbolism for mass markets (Fig. 140).

WHICH TECHNOLOGICAL REVOLUTION?

It is significant that the "advanced technology" favored by progressive Modern architecture continues to be even today that of mass production and industrialization, nineteenth-century style. Even Archigram's structural visions are Jules Verne versions of the Industrial Revolution with an appliqué of Pop-aerospace terminology (Fig. 141). However, the American aerospace industry itself, the chosen model of latter-day architectural megastructuralists, is facing its own trauma of extinction owing to oversize and overspecialization. As Peter Barnes in the *New Republic* suggests,[17]

"From a purely economic standpoint, the aerospace giants have become more of a burden to the nation than an asset. Despite the myriad promises that science holds in store, America does not now need any great new strides forward in technology, at least in the aerospace field. What it needs is breathing space, a chance to evaluate the impact of current technology and to distribute the fruits of progress more equitably. It needs to think small, not big."

According to Barnes, Boeing's "Operation Breakthrough" housing project required $7,750 per house unit in site-management costs alone, excluding costs of architectural services or construction.

The relevant revolution today is the current electronic one. Architecturally, the symbol systems that electronics purveys so well are more important than its engineering content. The most urgent technological problem facing us is the humane meshing of advanced scientific and technical systems with our imperfect and exploited human systems, a problem worthy of the best attention of architecture's scientific ideologues and visionaries.

For us the most boring pavilions at Expo '67 were those that corresponded to the progressive structures of nineteenth-century world's fairs celebrated by Sigfried Giedion; while the Czech Pavilion—an architectural and structural nonentity, but tatooed with symbols and moving pictures—was by far the most interesting. It also had the longest lines of spectators; the show, not the building, drew the crowd. The Czech Pavilion was almost a decorated shed.

PREINDUSTRIAL IMAGERY FOR A POSTINDUSTRIAL ERA

A language of preindustrial forms has complemented that of industrial forms in late Modern architecture. Le Corbusier's early sketches of Mediterranean villages probably initiated the preoccupation of Modern

17. Peter Barnes, "Aerospace Dinosaurs," *The New Republic*, March 27, 1971, p. 19.

architects and theorists with vernacular, indigenous, or anonymous architecture. The simple, planar geometry of white Mediterranean forms appealed to the Cubist-Purist aesthetic of the young Le Corbusier, and their bold, rude plasticity was transformed into the *béton brut* of his late work. Then *béton brut* became a style—*the* style after the post-Miesian reaction against frame and panel architecture, with a vocabulary of forms, not to mention an explicit system of porportions, the Modulor, as precise as those of the Renaissance orders.

Architects who have adapted the forms of La Tourette for heroic symbolic purposes far removed from their original meaning, in using them in precast units, brick and baked enamel, from the industrial parks of New Jersey to the architectural monuments of Tokyo, have also harked back to the Mediterranean handcraft vernacular that inspired La Tourette. Vernacular models are popular where advanced technology is, even for Modern architects, farfetched, that is, for individual houses in the suburbs. The acceptance of primitive vernacular architecture has let in traditional architecture by the back door in the name of "regionalism." Today even traditional American shed roofs and boards-and-battens are accepted and replace the flat roofs and imitation concrete that architects strove for and clients resisted in suburbia.

What architects now call anonymous architecture comes close to what we are calling Ordinary architecture, but it is not the same because it eschews symbolism and style. While architects have adapted the simple forms of vernacular architecture, they have largely ignored the complex symbolism behind them. They themselves have used the vernacular vocabularies symbolically, to suggest association with the past and simple, deterministic virtue, that is, as early examples of a correspondence between structural methods, social organization, and environmental influences, paralleling at a primitive level the benign processes that shape the industrial vernacular. Yet, ironically, architects—except for Aldo van Eyck in Africa and Gunther Nitschke in Japan—have discounted the symbolic values that invest these forms and dominate, so anthropologists tell us, the artifactual environment of primitive cultures, often contradicting function and structure in their influence on form.

FROM LA TOURETTE TO LEVITTOWN

It is a further irony that Modern architects, who can embrace vernacular architecture remote in place or time, can contemptuously reject the current vernacular of the United States, that is, the merchant builders' vernacular of Levittown and the commercial vernacular of Route 66. This aversion to the conventional building around us could be an exotic survival of nineteenth-century Romanticism, but we think it is merely that architects are able to discern the symbolism in the forms of their own vernacular. They are unable to discern, either through ignorance or detachment, the symbolism of Mykonos or the Dogon. They understand the symbolism of Levittown and do not like it, nor are they prepared to suspend judgment on it in order to learn and, by learning, to make subsequent judgment more sensitive (Fig. 142). The content of the symbols, commercial hucksterism and middle-middle-class social aspiration, is so distasteful to many architects that they are unable to investigate openmindedly the basis for the symbolism or to analyze the forms of suburbia for their functional value; indeed they find it difficult to concede that any "liberal" architect could do so.[18]

Architects who find middle-middle-class social aspirations distasteful and like uncluttered architectural form see only too well the symbolism in the suburban residential landscape—for instance, in its stylish "bi-levels" in the Regency, Williamsburg, New Orleans, French Provincial, or Prairie-Organic modes, and its ornamented ranches with carriage lanterns, mansards, and antiqued brick. They recognize the symbolism, but they do not accept it. To them the symbolic decoration of the split-level suburban sheds represents the debased, materialistic values of a consumer economy where people are brainwashed by mass marketing and have no choice but to move into the ticky-tacky, with its vulgar violations of the nature of materials and its visual pollution of architectural sensibilities, and surely, therefore, the ecology.

This viewpoint throws out the variety with the vulgarity. In dismissing the architectural value of the Strip, it discounts also its simple and commonsense functional organization, which meets the needs of our sensibilities in an automobile environment of big spaces and fast movement, including the need for explicit and heightened symbolism. Similarly, in suburbia, the eclectic ornament on and around each of the relatively small houses reaches out to you visually across the relatively big lawns and makes an impact that pure architectural articulation could never make, at least in time, before you have passed on to the next house. The lawn sculpture partway between the house and the curving curb acts as a visual booster within this space, linking the symbolic architecture to the moving vehicle. So sculptural jockeys, carriage lamps, wagon wheels, fancy house numbers, fragments of split-rail fences, and mailboxes on erect chains all have a spatial as well as a symbolic role. Their forms identify vast space as do the urns in Le Nôtre's parterres, the ruined temples in English parks, and the sign in the A&P parking lot (Fig. 143).

But the symbolic meanings of the forms in builder's vernacular also serve to identify and support the individualism of the owner. The occu-

18. This, perhaps, accounts for the fact that we have been called "Nixonites," "Reaganites," or the equivalent, by Roger Montgomery, Ulrich Franzen, Kenneth Frampton, and a whole graduating class of Cooper Union.

pant of an anonymous vernacular tenement on an Italian medieval street could achieve identity through decoration on a front door—or perhaps through the *bella figura* of clothing—within the scale of a spatially limited, foot-going community. The same held for families behind the unified facades of Nash's London terraces. But for the middle-class suburbanite living, not in an antebellum mansion, but in a smaller version lost in a large space, identity must come through symbolic treatment of the form of the house, either through styling provided by the developer (for instance, split-level Colonial) or through a variety of symbolic ornaments applied thereafter by the owner (the Rococo lamp in the picture window or the wagon wheel out front, Fig. 144).

The critics of suburban iconography attribute its infinite combinations of standard ornamental elements to clutter rather than variety. This can be dismissed by suburbia's connoisseurs as the insensitivity of the uninitiate. To call these artifacts of our culture crude is to be mistaken concerning scale. It is like condemning theater sets for being crude at five feet or condemning plaster *putti*, made to be seen high above a Baroque cornice, for lacking the refinements of a Mino da Fiesole bas-relief on a Renaissance tomb. Also, the boldness of the suburban doodads distracts the eye from the telephone poles that even the silent majority does not like.

SILENT-WHITE-MAJORITY ARCHITECTURE

Many people like suburbia. This is the compelling reason for learning from Levittown. The ultimate irony is that although Modern architecture from the start has claimed a strong social basis for its philosophy, Modern architects have worked to keep formal and social concerns separate rather than together. In dismissing Levittown, Modern architects, who have characteristically promoted the role of the social sciences in architecture, reject whole sets of dominant social patterns because they do not like the architectural consequences of these patterns. Conversely, by defining Levittown as "silent-white-majority" architecture, they reject it again because they do not like what they believe to be the silent white majority's political views. These architects reject the very heterogeneity of our society that makes the social sciences relevant to architecture in the first place. As Experts with Ideals, who pay lip service to the social sciences, they build for Man rather than for people—this means, to suit themselves, that is, to suit their own particular upper-middle-class values, which they assign to everyone. Most suburbanites reject the limited formal vocabularies architects' values promote, or accept them 20 years later modified by the tract builder: The Usonian house becomes the ranch house. Only the very poor, via public housing, are dominated by architects' values. Developers build for markets rather than for Man and probably do less harm than authoritarian architects would do if they had the developers' power.

One does not have to agree with hard-hat politics to support the rights of the middle-middle class to their own architectural aesthetics, and we have found that Levittown-type aesthetics are shared by most members of the middle-middle class, black as well as white, liberal as well as conservative. If analyzing suburbia's architecture implies that one has let the Nixon regime "penetrate even the field of architectural criticism,"[19] then the field of urban planning has been infiltrated by Nixonites for more than 10 years—by Abrams, Gans, Webber, Dyckman, and Davidoff. For our critique is nothing new; the social planners have been making it for more than a decade. But in this Nixon-silent-majority diatribe, especially in its architectural, as opposed to its racial and military, dimensions, there is a fine line between liberalism and old-fashioned class snobbery.

Another obvious point is that "visual pollution" (usually someone else's house or business) is not the same order of phenomenon as air and water pollution. You can like billboards without approving of strip mining in Appalachia. There is no "good" way to pollute land, air, or water. Sprawl and strip we can learn to do well. However, *Life* magazine, in an editorial entitled "Erasing Grown-Up Vandalism," equates suburban sprawl, billboards, wires, and gasoline stations with the strip mining that has despoiled too much of the country.[20] "Visual pollution" seems to inspire editorial writers and photographers, who view it with alarm, to poetic descriptions of it in the manner of Milton and Doré. Their style is often in direct conflict with their opprobrium. If it is all bad, why is it so inspiring?

SOCIAL ARCHITECTURE AND SYMBOLISM

We architects who hope for a reallocation of national resources toward social purposes must take care to lay emphasis on the purposes and their promotion rather than on the architecture that shelters them. This reorientation will call for ordinary architecture, not ducks. But when there is little money to spend on architecture, then surely greatest architectural imagination is required. Sources for modest buildings and images with social purpose will come, not from the industrial past, but from the everyday city around us, of modest buildings and modest spaces with symbolic appendages.

19. Ulrich Franzen, *Progressive Architecture*, Letter to the Editor (April 1970), p. 8.

20. *Life* (April 9, 1971), p. 34. Direct quotation was not permitted.

139. Recommendation for a monument

140. Mobile home, California City, California

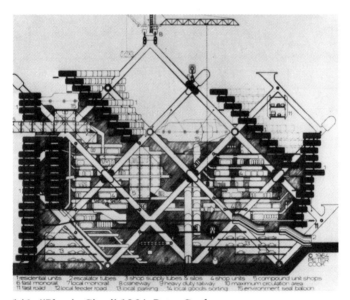

141. "Plug-in City," 1964; Peter Cook

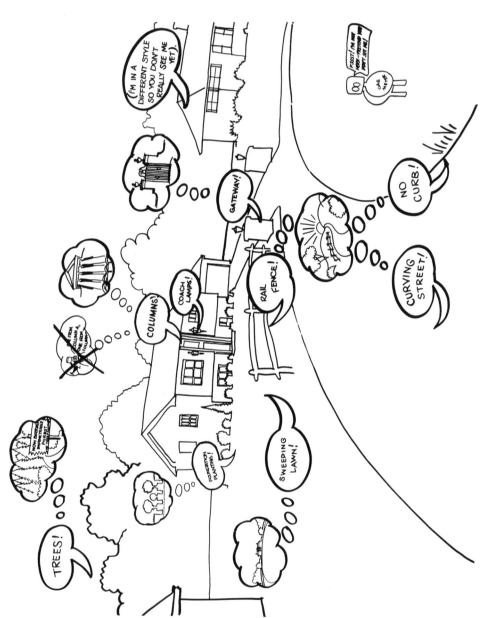

142. "Precedents of Suburban Symbols," Learning from Levittown studio, Yale, 1970

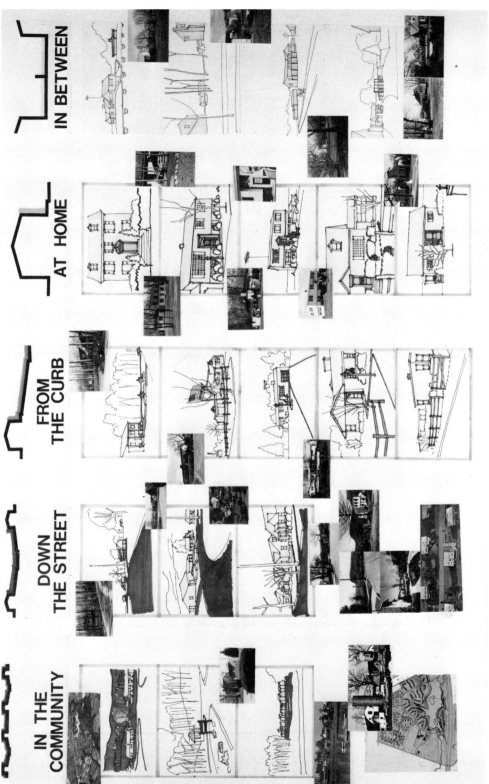

IN THE COMMUNITY   DOWN THE STREET   FROM THE CURB   AT HOME   IN BETWEEN

143. "Suburban Space, Sprawl, and Imagery," Learning from Levittown studio, Yale, 1970

144. Developer's house with applied symbols

145. Flamingo Hotel, Las Vegas

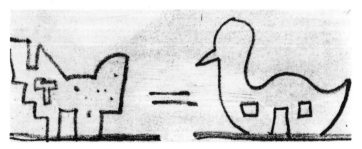

146. Minimegastructures are mostly ducks.

Meeting the architectural implications and the critical social issues of our era will require that we drop our involuted, architectural expressionism and our mistaken claim to be building outside a formal language and find formal languages suited to our times. These languages will incorporate symbolism and rhetorical appliqué. Revolutionary eras are given to didactic symbolism and to the propagandistic use of architecture to promote revolutionary aims. This is as true for the symbolism of today's ghetto rebuilders (African militant or middle-class conservative) as it was for the Romantic Roman republican symbolism of revolutionary France. Boullé was a propagandist and symbolist as well as a formalist. He saw, as we must see, architecture as symbol in space before form in space. To find our symbolism we must go to the suburban edges of the existing city that are symbolically rather than formalistically attractive and represent the aspirations of almost all Americans, including most low-income urban dwellers and most of the silent white majority. Then the archetypal Los Angeles will be our Rome and Las Vegas our Florence; and, like the archetypal grain elevator some generations ago, the Flamingo sign will be the model to shock our sensibilities towards a new architecture (Fig. 145).

HIGH-DESIGN ARCHITECTURE

Finally, learning from popular culture does not remove the architect from his or her status in high culture. But it may alter high culture to make it more sympathetic to current needs and issues. Because high culture and its cultists (last year's variety) are powerful in urban renewal and other establishment circles, we feel that people's architecture as the people want it (and not as some architect decides Man needs it) does not stand much chance against urban renewal until it hangs in the academy and therefore is acceptable to the decision makers. Helping this to happen is a not-reprehensible part of the role of the high-design architect; it provides, together with moral subversion through irony and the use of a joke to get to seriousness, the weapons of artists of nonauthoritarian temperament in social situations that do not agree with them. The architect becomes a jester.

Irony may be the tool with which to confront and combine divergent values in architecture for a pluralist society and to accommodate the differences in values that arise between architects and clients. Social classes rarely come together, but if they can make temporary alliances in the designing and building of multivalued community architecture, a sense of paradox and some irony and wit will be needed on all sides.

Understanding the content of Pop's messages and the way that it is projected does not mean that one need agree with, approve of, or reproduce that content. If the commercial persuasions that flash on the strip are materialistic manipulation and vapid subcommunication,[21] which cleverly appeal to our deeper drives but send them only superficial messages, it does not follow that we architects who learn from their techniques must reproduce the content or the superficiality of their messages. (But we *are* indebted to them for helping us to recognize that Modern architecture too has a content and a vapid one at that.) Just as Lichtenstein has borrowed the techniques and images of the comics to convey satire, sorrow, and irony rather than violent high adventure, so may the architect's high reader suggest sorrow, irony, love, the human condition, happiness, or merely the purpose within, rather than the necessity to buy soap or the possibility of an orgy. On the other hand, the interpretation and evaluation of symbolic content in architecture is an ambiguous process. The didactic symbolism of Chartres may represent to some the subtleties of medieval theology and to others the depths of medieval superstition or manipulation. Manipulation is not the monopoly of crass commercialism. And manipulation works both ways: Commercial interests and the billboard lobby manipulate, but so do cultural lobbies and design review boards, when they use their intimidating prestige to promote antisign legislation and beautification.

SUMMARY

The progressive, technological, vernacular, process-oriented, superficially socially concerned, heroic and original content of Modern architecture has been discussed before by critics and historians. Our point is that this content did not flow inevitably from the solving of functional problems but arose from Modern architects' unexplicated iconographic preferences and was manifest through a language—several languages—of form, and that formal languages and associational systems are inevitable and good, becoming tyrannies only when we are unconscious of them. Our other point is that the content of the unacknowledged symbolism of current Modern architecture is silly. We have been designing dead ducks.

We do not know if the time will come for serious architectural oceanographic urbanism, for example, as opposed to the present offshore posturing of the world futurist architectural visionaries. We suspect that one day it may, though hardly in the forms now envisioned. As practicing architects in the here and now, we do not have much interest in such predictions. We do know, however, that the chief resources of our society go into things with little architectural potential: war, electronic communication, outer space, and, to a much lesser extent, social serv-

---

21. Thomas Maldonado, *La speranza progettuale, ambiente e società*, Chapter 15, Nuovo Politecnico 35 (Turin: Einaudi, 1970).

ices. As we have said, this is not the time and ours is not the environment for heroic communication via pure architecture.

When Modern architects righteously abandoned ornament on buildings, they unconsciously designed buildings that *were* ornament. In promoting Space and Articulation over symbolism and ornament, they distorted the whole building into a duck. They substituted for the innocent and inexpensive practice of applied decoration on a conventional shed the rather cynical and expensive distortion of program and structure to promote a duck; minimegastructures are mostly ducks (Fig. 146). It is now time to reevaluate the once-horrifying statement of John Ruskin that architecture is the decoration of construction, but we should append the warning of Pugin: It is all right to decorate construction but never construct decoration.

APPENDIX:
ON DESIGN REVIEW BOARDS
AND FINE ARTS COMMISIONS

Excerpts from an interview, May 1971, with Professor Jesse Dukeminier, Law School, University of California, Los Angeles.

"Design Review Boards raise certain constitutional issues. Lawyers speak of them in terms of 'due process,' and 'equal protection of the law.' Due process means a fair hearing, and equal protection means no arbitrary discrimination. There are two ways to achieve these:
1. By building standards into the legal system.
2. Where the problem is not amenable to quantifying the standard, by building fairness into procedures, by requiring accountability in the exercise of discretion.

"There are certain standards that have long controlled the design of buildings. In zoning, for example, we have set-back lines, bulk controls, and height limitations. These are standards that an architect can work within because they really don't involve very much discretion, and every person who has ability is subjected to them. If these standards are laid down in advance by the City, one architect cannot say that he is particularly discriminated against, though he might disagree with the standard itself.

"Where we can't lay down standards, where the problem is not amenable to standards, we appoint a board and give it discretion. The Board must be accountable in the exercise of its discretion. We have in the American system of government various ways of making persons in power accountable for their actions. Judges, for example, have great discretion, but they have to write opinions. They can't rule for one party without saying why. They can be criticized when they have opened their minds for criticism by writing an opinion or giving an opinion. This is a great protection.

"From a legal point of view the heart of the problem with Design Review Boards is that:
1. There are no standards laid down to guide them.
2. They have broad discretion, and we have not built into the system any way of making them accountable for their actions."

The courts have ruled that beauty is an urban amenity to be sought through the police powers, review boards, and other regulatory measures; but they have omitted to set the standards by which beauty may be defined or the processes through which it may be equitably judged to be present. Local authorities have reacted by appointing "experts" (usually local architects) who use their own discretion in assigning beauty or lack of it to the works of others. The limits set on capriciousness, authoritarianism, or venality in such a system are those internal to the individual review board members. This is rule by man rather than rule by law.

In proceedings based solely on taste, the supplicant architect is left perplexed, and often thousands of dollars are lost in frustrating attempts, by scheming rather than designing, to anticipate or to follow the dicta of "experts" whose tastes and philosophies differ from the architect's own or are so capricious as to be incomprehensible.

Aesthetically, too, the aim is not achieved. Any artist could have told the lawmakers that you cannot legislate beauty and that attempts to do so by the use of experts will result not only in gross injustice but in an ugly deadness in the environment.

Beauty escapes in the pursuit of safety, which promotes a simplistic sameness over a varied vitality. It withers under the edicts of today's aging architectural revolutionaries who man the review boards and who have achieved aesthetic certainty.

BIBLIOGRAPHY

A. WRITINGS ABOUT VENTURI AND RAUCH

1960

"From Repainting to Redesign," *Architectural Forum*, January 1960, pp. 122-130. (Duke House, New York University.)

"NYU—Duke House," *Interiors*, March 1960, pp. 120-125.

1961

"New Talent USA—Architecture," *Art in America*, vol. 49, No. 1, 1961, p. 63. (Article concerns Robert Venturi; discusses 2 architectural projects.)

Rowan, Jan C., "Wanting to Be: The Philadelphia School," *Progressive Architecture*, April 1961, pp. 131-163.

1963

"FDR Memorial Competition: Discussion," *Casabella*, November 1963, pp. 12-13.

"High Style for a Campus Eatery," *Progressive Architecture*, December 1963, pp. 132-136. (Grand's Restaurant.)

1964

"Americans to Watch in 1964: Architecture—Robert Venturi," *Pageant*, February 1964, p. 72.

Moore, Charles, "Houses: The Architect Speaks to Man's Needs," *Progressive Architecture*, May 1964, pp. 124ff.

1965

Architectural League of New York: Architecture and the Arts Awards, 1965. (Venturi House: Honorable Mention.)

Charette—Pennsylvania Journal of Architecture, November 1965. (Cover: Venturi House.)

"Complexities and Contradictions," *Progressive Architecture*, May 1965, pp. 168-174.

Love, Nancy, "The Architectural Rat Race," *Greater Philadelphia Magazine*, December 1965, pp. 55ff.

Osborn, Michelle (in consultation with Romaldo Giurgola), "A Personal Kind of House," *The Philadelphia Evening Bulletin*, October 15, 1965, p. 55. (Venturi House.)

"Paths of Younger Architects," *The Philadelphia Inquirer Magazine*, March 3, 1965.

"Robert Venturi," *Arts and Architecture*, April 1965, p. 22.

"Venturi's Philadelphia Fountain Exemplifies Vernacular Urban Scale," *South Carolina AIA Review of Architecture*, 1965, pp. 29-31.

1966
"Are Young Architects Designing Prototypes of Your Future Models?" *American Builder*, October 1966, pp. 60-71. (Venturi House.)

"Dynamic Design with Angular Planes," *House and Garden Building Guide*, Spring/Summer 1966, pp. 132-135.

McCoy, Esther, "Young Architects: The Small Office," *Arts and Architecture*, February-March 1966, p. 28.

Scott Brown, Denise, "Team 10, Perspecta 10 and the Present State of Architectural Theory" (see Section C).

Scully, Vincent, "America's Architectural Nightmare: The Motorized Megalopolis," *Holiday*, March 1966, pp. 94ff.

Stern, Robert A. M., *40 under 40*, Architectural League of New York, 1966. (Catalog for exhibit at the Architectural League of New York.)

_____, "Review of *L'architecture d'aujourd'hui* Issue on USA '65," *Progressive Architecture*, May 1966, pp. 256, 266.

"Venturi House—'Mannerist'," *Architectural Review*, February 1966, p. 49.

1967
Blake, Peter, *Architectural Forum*, June 1967, pp. 56-57. (Review of *Complexity and Contradiction in Architecture*; discussion, July 1967, p. 16.)

Colquhoun, Alan, "Robert Venturi," *Architectural Design*, August 1967, p. 362.

"Fourteenth Annual Design Awards," *Progressive Architecture*, January 1967, pp. 144-154.

Journal of the American Institute of Architects, June 1967, p. 94. (Review of *Complexity and Contradiction*.)

"Maison R. Venturi," *L'Architecture d'aujourd'hui*, January 1967, p. 26.

Miller, N., *Journal of the Society of Architectural Historians*, December 1967, pp. 381-389. (Review of *Complexity and Contradiction*.)

"New-Old Guild House Apartments," *Progressive Architecture*, May 1967, pp. 133-137.

"New Schools for New Towns," *Design Fete IV*, School of Architecture, Rice University, Houston, Texas, 1967.

Pile, J. F., *Interiors*, July 1967, p. 24. (Review of *Complexity and Contradiction*.)

Ramsgard, Birgitte, "Complexity and Contradiction" ("Om Kompleksitet i Arkitektinen"), *Arkitekten*, 1967, pp. 608-609.

Rykwert, J., *Domus*, August 1967, p. 23. (Review of *Complexity and Contradiction*.)

"The Permissiveness of Supermannerism," *Progressive Architecture*, October 1967, pp. 169-173.

"Three Projects," *Perspecta 11*, 1967, pp. 103-111.

Wellemeyer, Marilyn, "An Inspired Renaissance in Indiana," *Life*, November 17, 1967, pp. 74-84.

Whiffen, M., *Journal of the Society of Architectural Historians*, October 1967, pp. 198-199. (Review of *Complexity and Contradiction*.)

"Young American Architects," *Zodiac 17*, 1967, pp. 138-151.

1968

Bottero, Maria, "Passanto e presente nell'architettura 'pop' Americana," *Communità*, December 1968.

"L'Architecture en tant qu'espace, l'architecture en tant que symbole," *L'Architecture d'aujourd'hui*, September 1968, pp. 36-37.

"Less is Bore," *Toshi-Jukatu: A Monthly Journal of Urban Housing*, June 1968, pp. 42-46ff.

Lobell, John, "Both-And: A New Architectural Concept," *Arts*, February 1968, pp. 12-13.

McCoy, Esther, "Buildings in the United States," *Lotus*, vol. 4, 1967/8, pp. 15-123.

Norberg-Schulz, Christian, "Less or More?," *Architectural Review*, April 1968, p. 257-258.

Osborn, Michelle, "Dilemma in a Time of Change," *The Philadelphia Evening Bulletin*, April 26, 1968. (Brighton Beach.)

"Pop Architecture," *Architecture Canada*, October 1968.

Record of Submissions and Awards, Competition for Middle Income Housing at Brighton Beach, HDA, City of New York, Brooklyn, 1968. (Jury comments.)

"Two New Buildings by Venturi and Rauch," *Progressive Architecture*, November 1968, pp. 116-123. (Fire Station #4, Columbus, Indiana, and the Medical Office Building, Bridgeton, N.J.)

1969

Berson, Lenore, "South Street Insurrection," *Philadelphia Magazine*, September 1969, pp. 87-91ff.

"Education and Extension," *Art Gallery of Ontario Annual Report 1969-70*. (On Bauhaus Lectures by Venturi.)

Huxtable, Ada Louise, "The Case for Chaos," *The New York Times*, January 26, 1969, Section 2. Reprinted in *Will They Ever Finish Bruckner Boulevard?*, 1970.

Jencks, Charles, "Points of View," *Architectural Design*, December 1969. (Football Hall of Fame.)

Jenson, Robert, "Resort Hotels: Symbols and Associations in Their Design," *Architectural Record*, December 1969, pp. 119-123.

Love, Nancy, "The Deflatable Fair," *Philadelphia Magazine*, April 1969, pp. 137-140. (Denise Scott Brown and Robert Venturi on the Bicentennial.)

Richard, Paul, "Learning from Las Vegas," *The Washington Post*, January 19, 1969, The Arts, pp. k1, k8.

_____ , "Learning from Las Vegas," *Today's Family Digest*, November 1969, pp. 12-17.

Scully, Vincent, "A Search for Principle Between Two Wars," *Journal of the Royal Institute of British Architects*, June 1969, pp. 240-247. (A discussion of architectural aesthetics, philosophy, etc., with reference to Venturi.)

_____, *American Architecture and Urbanism.* New York: Frederick A. Praeger, Inc., 1969.

Stern, Robert A. M., *New Directions in American Architecture.* New York: George Braziller, 1969. (Chapter on Venturi, pp. 50-59.)

Watson, Donald, "LLV, LLV:? VVV," *Novum Organum 5.* New Haven: Yale School of Art and Architecture, 1969. (Review of Las Vegas studio.)

Wolfe, Tom, "Electrographic Architecture," *Architectural Design*, July 1969, pp. 380-382.

1970

"A Question of Values," *American Heritage*, August 1970, p. 119. (On planning for South Street.)

"Academic Village: State University College, Purchase, New York; Social Science and Humanities Building," *Architectural Forum*, November 1970, pp. 38-39.

Annual Report 1970 of the Director of University Development, Yale University, New Haven, Connecticut, 1970, pp. 19-23. (Yale Mathematics Building.)

Berkeley, Ellen Perry, "Mathematics at Yale," *Architectural Forum*, July/August 1970, pp. 62-67. See readers' response, October 1970.

Berson, Lenore, "Dreams for a New South Street are Spun at Theatre Meetings," *Center City Philadelphia*, February 1970.

"Choosing a Non-Monument," *Architectural Forum*, June 1970, p. 22. (Yale Mathematics Building.)

"Competition-Winning Building to Provide Yale Mathematicians with New Quarters," *Journal of the American Institute of Architects*, July 1970, p. 8.

"Co-op City Controversy," *Progressive Architecture*, April 1970, p. 9. (See also letters to the editor on "Co-op City: Learning to Like It," ibid., February 1970.)

Davis, Douglas, "Architect of Joy," *Newsweek*, November 2, 1970, pp. 103-106. (Article about Morris Lapidus.)

Eberhard, John P., "American Architecture and Urbanism," *Journal of the American Institute of Architects*, August 1970, pp. 64-66.

Huxtable, Ada Louise, "Heroics are Out, Ordinary is In," *The New York Times*, January 18, 1970, Section 2.

_____ , *Will They Ever Finish Bruckner Boulevard?*, New York: Macmillan Company, 1970, pp. 186-187.

"In Defense of the Strip," *Journal of the American Institute of Architects*, December 1970, p. 64. (On Las Vegas.)

Jacobs, Jay, "A Commitment to Excellence," *The Art Gallery*, December 1970, pp. 17-32.

Kurtz, Stephen A., "Toward an Urban Vernacular," *Progressive Architecture*, July 1970, pp. 100-105.

"Mathematics at Yale: Readers' Response," *Architectural Forum*, October 1970, pp. 64-66. See also "Your Point of View," *Progressive Architecture*, November 1970.

"Ordinary as Artform," *Progressive Architecture*, April 1970, pp. 106-109. (Lieb House.)

Osborn, Michelle, "The Ugly American Architect," *Philadelphia Magazine*, April 1970, pp. 52-56.

Pawley, Martin, "Leading from the Rear," *Architectural Design*, January 1970, p. 45. (See also reply to Pawley, *Architectural Design*, July 1970.)

Reif, Rita, "A Family Who Built a 'Real Dumb House' in a 'Banal Environment'," *The New York Times*, August 17, 1970, p. 22L. (Lieb House.)

"Saint Francis de Sales Church," *Liturgical Arts*, August 1970, pp. 124-126.

Schulze, Franz, "Chaos as Architecture," *Art in America*, July/August 1970, pp. 88-96. (Discussion of the philosophy and work of Venturi and Rauch. Reply, November 1970.)

"Seventeenth Annual Progressive Architecture Design Awards," *Progressive Architecture*, January 1970, pp. 76-135. (Robert Venturi juror.)

Sica, Paolo, *L'immagine della città da Sparta a Las Vegas*. Bari: Laterza, 1970.

Smith, C. Ray, "Electric Demolition, A Milestone in Church Art: St. Francis de Sales, Philadelphia," *Progressive Architecture*, September 1970, pp. 92-95.

"Zoning Rebuilds the Theatre," *Progressive Architecture*, December 1970, pp. 76ff.

1971

"A House on Long Beach Island," *International Asbestos Cement Review*, April 1971, pp. 6-8.

Architecture for the Arts: The State University of New York College at Purchase. New York: The Museum of Modern Art, 1971.

Cliff, Ursula, "Are the Venturis Putting Us On?" *Design and Environment*, Summer 1971, pp. 52-59ff.

Davis, Douglas, "New Architecture: Building for Man," *Newsweek*, April 19, 1971, pp. 78-90.

Eisenman, Peter, et al., "The City as an Artifact," *Casabella*, Vol. 35, No. 359/360, December 1971. (See articles by Eisenman, Rykwert, Ellis, Anderson, Schumacher, and Frampton, and reply by Scott Brown.)

Glueck, Grace, "Don't Knock Sprawl," *The New York Times*, October 10, 1971, p. 16D.

Goldberger, Paul, "Less is More—Mies van der Rohe. Less is a Bore—Robert Venturi," *The New York Times Magazine*, October 19, 1971, pp. 34-37ff.

Goodman, Robert. *After the Planners*. New York: Simon & Schuster, 1971.

Huxtable, Ada Louise, "Celebrating 'Dumb, Ordinary' Architecture," *The New York Times*, October 1, 1971, p. 43.

_____, "Plastic Flowers are Almost All Right," *The New York Times*, October 10, 1971, p. 22D.

Jensen, Robert, "Images for a New Cal City," *Architectural Record*, June 1971, pp. 117-120.

Kauffman, Herbert H., "A Sophisticated Setting for Two Suburban G.P.'s," *Medical Economics*, December 6, 1971, pp. 88-90.

Kay, June Holtz, "Champions of Messy Vitality," *The Boston Sunday Globe*, October 24, 1971, p. 25A.

McLaughlin, Patsy, "Ms. Scott Brown Keeps Her Own Taste to Herself," *The Pennsylvania Gazette*, December 1971, p. 38.

Nelson, Nels, "Bonkers Over Billboards—and Very Cereus," *The Philadelphia Daily News*, September 24, 1971, p. 3F.

Osborn, Michelle, "The Crosstown is Dead. Long Live the Crosstown," *Architectural Forum*, October 1971, pp. 38-42.

Papachristou, Tician, and James Stewart Polshek, "Venturi: Style, not Substance," *The New York Times*, November 14, 1971, p. 24D.

"Robert Venturi," *Architecture and Urbanism*, Japan, October 1971. (Issue devoted to the work of Venturi and Rauch.)

"Robert Venturi," *Kenchiku Bunka*, March 1971, pp. 84-94.

Scully, Vincent, "The Work of Venturi and Rauch, Architects and Planners," Whitney Museum of American Art, September 1971. (Exhibit pamphlet.)

"Venturi and Rauch," *L'architecture d'aujourd'hui*, December-January 1971-1972, pp. 84-104 and cover. (Plans 1964-1970; Yale Mathematics Building; Trubek and Wislocki houses; Crosstown Community; California City.)

"Venturi and Rauch Projects Shown in New York," *Architectural Record*, November 1971, p. 37.

Vrchota, Janet, "Bye, Bye Bauhaus," *Print*, September/October 1971, pp. 66-67. (On Venturi and Rauch exhibit at Whitney Museum.)

"Yale Mathematics Building," *Architectural Design*, February 1971, p. 115.

1972

"Aprendiendo de Todas Las Cosas," *Arte Y Comento*, Bilbao, November 20, 1972.

"Arquitectura Pop," *El Comercio*, Lima, Aberlardo Oquerdo, April 16, 1972. (Review of *Aprendiendo*.)

Blasi, Cesare and Gabriella, "Venturi," *Casabella*, No. 364, April 1972, pp. 15-19.

"Brown, D.S., y Venturi, R.; 'Aprendiendo de Todas Las Cosas'," *ABC*, Miguel Perer Ferrero, Madrid, April 26, 1972.

Corrigan, Peter, "Reflection on a New American Architecture: The Venturis," *Architecture in Australia*, February 1972, pp. 55-66.

Cuadernos de Arquitectura, Barcelona, January 1972. (Review of *Aprendiendo*.)

Davis, Douglas, "From Forum to Strip," *Newsweek*, October 1972, p. 38.

Donohoe, Victoria, "Buildings: Good and Bad," *The Philadelphia Inquirer*, June 30, 1972, p. 18.

Drew, Philip, *Third Generation: The Changing Meaning of Architecture*. New York: Praeger Publishers, 1972, pp. 35, 42, 48, 152ff, 160,

162. Published in German as *Die Dritte Generation: Architektur zwishen Produkt und Prozess.* Stuttgart: Verlag Gerd Hatje, 1972.

Flanagan, Barbara, "Venturi and Venturi, Architectural Anti-Heroes," *34th Street Magazine,* April 13, 1972, pp. 1, 4.

Friedman, Mildred S., ed., "Urban Redevelopment: 19th Century Vision, 20th Century Version," *Design Quarterly,* no. 85, 1972.

Groat, Linda, "Interview: Denise Scott Brown," *Networks 1,* California Institute of the Arts, 1972, pp. 49-55.

Hoffman, Donald, "Monuments and the Strip," *The Kansas City Star,* December 10, 1972, p. 1D. (Review of *Learning from Las Vegas.*)

Holmes, Ann, "Art Circles," *Houston Chronicle,* May 7, 1972.

Huxtable, Ada Louise, "Architecture in '71: Lively Confusion," *The New York Times,* January 4, 1972, p. 26L.

Jackson, J. B., "An Architect Learns from Las Vegas," *The Harvard Independent,* November 30, 1972.

Jellinek, Roger, "In Praise (!) of Las Vegas," *The New York Times,* Books of the Times, December 29, 1972, p. 23L.

"Learning from Las Vegas by Robert Venturi, Denise Scott Brown and Steven Izenour," *The New Republic,* Book Reviews, December 2, 1972.

Maldonado, Thomas. *La Speranza progettuale, ambiente e società,* Nuovo Politeenico 35. Turin: Einaudi, 1970. In English, *Design, Nature, and Revolution, Toward a Critical Ecology,* trans. Mario Domandi. New York: Harper & Row, 1972.

Marvel, Bill, "Can McDonald's, Chartres Find Happiness?" *The Miami Herald,* February 20, 1972, pp. 49K-50K.

——, "Do You Like the Arches? Sure, Easy, I Love Them!" *The National Observer,* February 12, 1972, pp. 1, 24.

McQuade, Walter, "Giving Them What They Want: The Venturi Influence," *Life Magazine,* April 14, 1972, p. 17.

Plous, Phyllis, "The Architecture of Venturi and Rauch," *Artweek,* Santa Barbara, November 1972, p. 3.

"Renovation of St. Francis de Sales, Philadelphia, 1968," *Architectural Design,* June 1972, p. 379.

Robinson, Lydia, "Learning from Las Vegas," *The Harvard Crimson,* December 4, 1972, p. 2.

Schwartz, Marty, "Radical-Radical Confrontation: I.V. Is Almost All Right," *UCSB Daily News*, November 16, 1972, p. 5.

Sealander, John. "Appreciating the Architectural UGLY," *The Highlander*, University of California at Riverside, November 30, 1972.

"Unas notas sobre, 'Aprendiendo de todas las cosas,' de Robert Venturi," Gerardo Delgado, Jose Ramon Sierra, *El Correo de Andalusia*, May 2, 1972.

"Un diseño per al consumisme," *Serra D'Or*, Oriul Bohigas, February 1972, p. 18. (Review of *Aprendiendo*.)

Vandevanter, Peter, "Unorthodox Architect," *Princeton Alumni Weekly*, Alumni Adventures, December 12, 1972, p. 15.

————, "Venturi: Controversial Philadelphia Architect," *The Daily Princetonian*, February 26, 1972, p. 5ff.

Vermel, Ann, *On the Scene*, Hartford Stage Company, January 1972, pp. 1-2.

Waroff, Deborah, "The Venturis—American Selection," *Building Design*, no. 113, August 4, 1972, pp. 12-13.

Wines, James, "The Case for the Big Duck: Another View," *Architectural Forum*, April 1972, pp. 60-61, 72.

1973

"Award of Merit," *House and Home*, May 1973, pp. 116-117.

"Best Houses of 1973," *American Home*, September 1973, p. 52.

Blanton, John, "Learning from Las Vegas," *Journal of the American Institute of Architects*, February 1973, pp. 56ff.

Carney, Francis, "The Summa Popologica of Robert ('Call Me Vegas') Venturi," *Journal of the Royal Institute of British Architects*, May 1973, pp. 242-244.

Cook, John W. and Klotz, Heinrich, *Conversations With Architects*. New York: Praeger Publishers, Inc., 1973. Interview with Robert Venturi and Denise Scott Brown, reprinted as "Ugly is Beautiful: The Main Street School of Architecture," *The Atlantic Monthly*, May 1973, pp. 33-43.

"En Passant Par Las Vegas," *Architecture, Mouvement, Continuité*, September 1973, pp. 28-34. (Review of *Learning from Las Vegas*.)

Fowler, Sigrid H., "Learning from Las Vegas," *Journal of Popular Culture*, Vol. 7, No. 2, 1973, pp. 425-433.

French, Philip, "The World's Most Celebrated Oasis," *The Times* (London), February 26, 1973. (Review of *Learning from Las Vegas.*)

Glixon, Neil, "Is This Art?" *Scholastic Voice*, November 29, 1973, pp. 2-8.

Hack, Gary, "Venturi View of the Strip Leads to Las Vagueness," *Landscape Architecture*, July 1973, pp. 376-378.

Holland, Laurence B., "Rear-guard Rebellion," *The Yale Review*, Spring 1973, pp. 456-461. (Review of *Learning from Las Vegas.*)

Huxtable, Ada Louise, "In Love with Times Square," *The New York Review of Books*, October 18, 1973, pp. 45-48. (Review of *Learning from Las Vegas.*)

Kemper, Alfred M., Sam Mori, and Jacqueline Thompson, *Drawings by American Architects*, New York: John Wiley and Sons, 1973, pp. 564-567.

Kurtz, Stephen A., *Wasteland: Building the American Dream.* New York: Praeger Publishers, 1973, pp. 11ff.

Levine, Stuart G., "Architectural Populism," *American Studies* (urban issue), Spring 1973, pp. 135-136. (Review of *Learning from Las Vegas.*)

McCoy, Esther, "Learning from Las Vegas," *Historic Preservation*, January-March 1973, pp. 44-46.

Matsushita, Kazuyuki, "Learning from Las Vegas," *Architecture and Urbanism*, Japan, April 1973, p. 116.

Merkel, Jayne, "Las Vegas as Architecture," *The Cincinnati Enquirer*, December 16, 1973, p. 6-G.

Moore, Charles, "Learning from Adam's House," *Architectural Record*, August 1973, p. 43. (Review of *Learning from Las Vegas.*)

Neil, J. Meredith, "Las Vegas on My Mind," *Journal of Popular Culture*, Vol. 7, No. 2, 1973, pp. 379-386.

Neuman, David J., "Learning from Las Vegas," *Journal of Popular Culture*, Spring 1973, p. 873.

Pawley, Martin, "Miraculous Expanding Tits versus Lacquered Nipples," *Architectural Design*, February 1973, p. 80. (Review of *Learning from Las Vegas.*)

Silver, Nathan, "Learning from Las Vegas," *The New York Times Book Review*, April 29, 1973, pp. 5-6.

"Some Decorated Sheds or Towards an Old Architecture," *Progressive Architecture*, May 1973, pp. 86-89.

Stern, Robert, "Stompin' at the Savoye," *Architectural Forum*, May 1973, pp. 46-48.

"Strip Building," *Times Literary Supplement*, April 6, 1973, p. 366.

von Moos, Stanislaus, "Learning from Las Vegas/Venturi et al.," *Neue Züricher Zeitung,* September 1973.

Wolf, Gary, Review of *Learning from Las Vegas, Journal of the Society of Architectural Historians*, October 1973, pp. 258-260.

Wright, L., "Robert Venturi and Anti-Architecture," *Architectural Review*, April 1973, pp. 262-264.

1974

"A Pair of Seaside Summer Cottages," *Second Home*, Spring-Summer 1974, pp. 68-71.

Allen, Gerald, "Venturi and Rauch's Humanities Building for the Purchase Campus of the State University of New York," *Architectural Record*, October 1974, pp. 120-124.

Batt, Margaret, "Historical Foundation Picks Strand Planners," *The Galveston Daily News*, Sunday, November 24, 1974, p. 1.

Beardsley, Monroe, "Learning from Las Vegas," *The Journal of Aesthetics and Art Criticism*, Winter 1974, pp. 245-246.

Cambell, Robert, "Yale Sums Up State of the Arts," *The Boston Globe*, Sunday, December 22, 1974, p. 26A.

Ciucci, Giorgio, "Walt Disney World," *Architecture, Mouvement, Continuité*, December 1974, pp. 42-51.

Cohen, Stuart, "Physical Context/Cultural Context: Including It All," *Oppositions 2*, January 4, 1974, pp. 1-40.

DeSeta, Cesare, "Robert Venturi, dissacratore e provocatore," *Casabella*, No. 394, October 1974, pp. 2-5.

Faghih, Nasrine, "Sémiologie du signe sans message," *Architecture, Mouvement, Continuité*, December 1974, pp. 35-40.

Farney, Dennis, "The School of 'Messy Vitality'," *The Wall Street Journal*, January 4, 1974, p. 20.

Fitch, James Marston, "Single Point Perspective," *Architectural Forum*, March 1974. (Review of *Learning from Las Vegas*.)

Garau, Piero, "Robert Venturi: architetto della strada," *Americana*, May-June 1974, pp. 37-40.

Hall, Peter, "*Learning from Las Vegas*," *Regional Studies*, Vol. 8, No. 1, 1974, pp. 98-99. (Review.)

Hine, Thomas, "City Planners Often Forget That People Must Live There," *The Philadelphia Inquirer*, May 6, 1974, p. 11E.

————, "Franklin Shrine to Center on Abstract 'Ghost' House," *Philadelphia Inquirer*, July 19, 1974, pp. 1-D, 3-D.

————, "Learning from Levittown's Suburban Sprawl," *The Philadelphia Inquirer*, February 17, 1974, Section H,I.

Holmes, Ann, "The Pop Artist Who Isn't Kidding Plans to Give Vitality to the Strand," *Houston Chronicle*, Sunday, November 24, 1974, Part A, Section 4.

Kay, Jane Holtz, "Learning from Las Vegas," *The Nation*, January 12, 1974.

Koetter, Fred, "On Robert Venturi, Denise Scott Brown and Steven Izenour's *Learning from Las Vegas*," *Oppositions 3*, May 1974, pp. 98-104.

Kramer, Paul R., "Wir lernen vom Rom und Las Vegas," *Werk, Architektur und Kunst*, February 1974, pp. 202-212. (Interview with Robert Venturi.)

Kuhns, William, "Learning from Las Vegas," *New Orleans Review*, Fall 1974, p. 394.

Moore, Charles W., and Nicholas Pyle, eds., *The Yale Mathematics Building Competition*. New Haven and London: Yale University Press, 1974.

Navone, Paola and Bruno Orlandoni, *Architettura "radicale."* Milan: Casabella, 1974, pp. 33ff.

"Nears Final Design," *The Hartford Times*, June 1974. (Hartford Stage Company.)

Raynor, Vivien, "Women in Professions, Architecture," *VIVA*, May 1974, pp. 30-31.

Redini, Maria Caterina, and Carla Saggioro, "Il tema della decorazione architettonica nell'America degli anni '60 attraverso *Perspecta, The*

Yale Architectural Journal," *Rassegna dell'Istituto di architettura e urbanistica*, University of Rome, August-December, 1974, pp. 99-125.

Schmertz, Mildred F., "Vincent Scully versus Charles Moore," *Architectural Record*, December 1974, p. 45.

Schulze, Franz, "Toward an 'Impure' Architecture," *Dialogue*, Vol. 7, No. 3, 1974, pp. 54-63.

Scully, Vincent, *The Shingle Style Today*. New York: Braziller, 1974.

Sky, Alison, "On Iconology," *On Site 5/6 On Energy*, 1974. (Interview with Denise Scott Brown.)

Sorkin, Michael, "Robert Venturi and the Function of Architecture at the Present Time," *Architectural Association Quarterly*, Vol. 6, No. 2, 1974, pp. 31-35. (See also letters in Vol. 7, No. 1.)

Tafuri, Manfredo, "L'Architecture dans le boudoir: The Language of Criticism and the Criticism of Language," *Oppositions 3*, May 1974, pp. 37-62.

Treu, Piera Gentile, *Della complessità in architettura: Problemi di composizione urbana nella teorica di Robert Venturi*. Padua: Tipografia "La Garangola," 1974.

"21st Awards Program: A Year of Issues," *Progressive Architecture*, January 1974, pp. 52-89. (Denise Scott Brown juror.)

"Venturi," *Architecture Plus*, March/April 1974, p. 80.

"Venturi and Rauch 1970-74," *Architecture and Urbanism*, Japan, November 1974. (Issue devoted to the work of Venturi and Rauch.)

Zobl, Engelbert, "Architektur USA—East II: Robert Venturi—John Rauch," *Architektur Aktuell—Fach Journal*, April 1974, pp. 17-18.

1975

Berliner, Donna Israel and David C., "Thirty-six Women with Real Power Who Can Help You," *Cosmopolitan*, April 1975, pp. 195-196.

Goldberger, Paul, "Tract House, Celebrated," *The New York Times Magazine*, September 14, 1975, pp. 68-69, 74. (On the Brant house.)

Hine, Thomas, "East Poplar's Curious 'Victory'," *Philadelphia Inquirer*, June 29, 1975. (Fairmount Manor and Poplar Community project.)

———, "Pretzel-Land Welcomes the World," *The Philadelphia In-*

quirer, Today Magazine, Sunday, April 13, 1975, pp. 35-42. (On the City Edges Project.)

Polak, Maralyn Lois, "Architect for Pop Culture," *The Philadelphia Inquirer*, Today Magazine, June 8, 1975, p. 8. (Interview with Denise Scott Brown.)

"Robert Venturi," *Current Biography*, July, 1975.

Rykwert, Joseph, "Ornament is No Crime," *Studio*, September 1975, pp. 95-97.

von Moos, Stanislaus, "Las Vegas, et cetera," and "Lachen, um nicht zu weinen," with French translation, *Archithese 13*, 1975, pp. 5-32.

1976

Beck, Haig, "Letter from London," *Architectural Design*, February 1976, p. 121.

Dixon, John, "Show Us the Way," editorial, *Progressive Architecture*, June 1976. See also "Views" and "News Report: Scully Refuses AIA Honors," pp. 6, 8, 32, 39.

Forgey, Benjamin, "Keeping the Cities' Insight," *The Washington Star*, February 29, 1976, pp. 1, 24c. (Review of "Signs of Life: Symbols in the American City," a Bicentennial exhibition, Renwick Gallery, National Collection of Fine Arts of the Smithsonian Institution, Washington, D.C.)

"Franklin Court," *Progressive Architecture*, April 1976, pp. 69-70. (This issue is devoted to the "Philadelphia Story"; Venturi and Rauch mentioned throughout.)

Futagawa, Yukio (editor and photographer), *Global Architecture 39: Venturi and Rauch*, Tokyo: A.D.A. EDITA, 1976. (Text by Paul Goldberger.)

Geddes, Jean, "Is Your House Crawling with Urban Symbolism?", *Forecast*, May 1976, pp. 40-41. (Review of "Signs of Life" exhibit.)

Hess, Thomas B., "White Slave Traffic," *New York*, April 5, 1976, pp. 62-63. (Review of "200 Years of American Sculpture," Whitney Museum, 1976.)

Hoelterhoff, Manuela, "A Little of Everything at the Whitney," *The Wall Street Journal*, June 9, 1976.

Hoffman, Donald, "Art Talk," *The Kansas City Star*, Feburary 8, 1976, p. 3D. (Exhibition at Kansas City Art Institute.)

Hughes, Robert, "Overdressing for the Occasion," *Time*, April 5, 1976, pp. 42, 47. (Review of "200 Years of American Sculpture.")

Huxtable, Ada Louise, "The Fall and Rise of Main Street," *The New York Times Magazine*, May 30, 1976, pp. 12-14. (Includes Galveston project.)

_____, "The Gospel According to Giedion and Gropius is under Attack," *The New York Times*, June 27, 1976, pp. 1, 29, Section 2.

_____, "The Pop World of the Strip and the Sprawl," *The New York Times*, March 21, 1976, p. 28D. (Review of "Signs of Life.")

Kleihues, Josef Paul (Organizer), *Dortmunder Architekturausstellung 1976*. Dortmund: Dortmunder Architekturhefte No. 3, 1976. (Catalog of an architecture exhibition that includes work of Venturi and Rauch.)

Kramer, Hilton, "A Monumental Muddle of American Sculpture," *The New York Times*, March 28, 1976, pp. 1, 34D. (Review of "200 Years of American Sculpture.")

Kron, Joan, "Photo Finishes," *New York*, March 22, 1976, pp. 56-57.

Lebensztejn, Jean-Claude, "Hyperéalisme, Kitsch et 'Venturi'," *Critique*, February 1976, pp. 99-135.

Lipstadt, Hélène R., "Interview with R. Venturi and D. Scott Brown," *Architecture, Mouvement, Continuité*, in press.

Marvel, Bill, "On Reading the American Cityscape," *National Observer*, April 19, 1976. (Review of "Signs of Life.")

Miller, Robert L., "New Haven's Dixwell Fire Station by Venturi and Rauch," *Architectural Record*, June 1976, pp. 111-116.

Morton, David, "Venturi and Rauch, Brant House, Greenwich, Conn.," *Progressive Architecture*, August 1976, pp. 50-53.

"Off the Skyline and into the Museum," *Newsday*, April 14, 1976, pp. 4-5 A.

Orth, Maureen, with Lucy Howard, "Schlock Is Beautiful," *Newsweek*, March 8, 1976, p. 56. (Review of "Signs of Life.")

Pfister, Harold, "Exhibitions," *The Decorative Arts Newsletter*, Society of Architectural Historians, Summer 1976, pp. 3-5.

Quinn, Jim, "Dumb is Beautiful," "Learning from Our Living Rooms," *Philadelphia Magazine*, October 1976, pp. 156ff.

Quinn, Michael C., and Paul H. Tucker, "Dixwell Fire Station," *Drawings for Modern Public Architecture in New Haven*. New Haven: Yale University Art Gallery, 1976, pp. 19-24. (Exhibition catalog.)

Reichlin, Bruno, and Martin Steinman, eds., *Archithese 19*, issue on Realism.

Richard, Paul, "Rooms with a View on Life," *The Washington Post*, April 13, 1976, pp. 1-2 B. (Review of "Signs of Life.")

Rosenblatt, Roger, "The Pure Soldier," *The New Republic*, March 27, 1976, p. 32. (Musings on "Signs of Life.")

Russell, Beverly, "Real Life: It's Beautiful," *House and Garden*, August 1976, pp. 79ff.

Ryan, Barbara Haddad, "Gaudy Reality of American Landscape Shines in Renwick Show," *Denver Post*, May 9, 1976. (Review of "Signs of Life.")

Stein, Benjamin, "The Art Forms of Everyday Life," *The Wall Street Journal*, April 22, 1976. (Review of "Signs of Life.")

Stephens, Suzanne, "Signs and Symbols as Show Stoppers," *Progressive Architecture*, May 1976, p. 37. (Review of "Signs of Life.")

"Symbols," *The New Yorker*, March 15, 1976, pp. 27-29. ("Signs of Life.")

Von Eckhardt, Wolf, "Signs of an Urban Vernacular," *The Washington Post*, February 28, 1976, pp. 1, 3C. (Review of "Signs of Life.")

Von Moos, S., "Americana: Zwei Ausstellungen in Washington," *Nene Zürcher Zeitung*, July 17-18, 1976. (Review of "Signs of Life.")

B. WRITINGS BY ROBERT VENTURI

1953
"The Campidoglio: A Case Study," *The Architectural Review*, May 1953, pp. 333-334.

1960
"Project for a Beach House," *Architectural Design*, November 1960.

1961
"Weekend House," *Progressive Architecture*, April 1961, pp. 156-157.

1965
"A Justification for a Pop Architecture," *Arts and Architecture*, April 1965, p. 22.

"Complexity and Contradiction in Architecture," *Perspecta 9-10*, 1965, pp. 17-56. (Extract.)

1966
Complexity and Contradiction In Architecture. New York: Museum of Modern Art and Graham Foundation, 1966. Translated into Japanese, 1969; into French, 1971; into Spanish, 1972.

1967
"Selection from: Complexity and Contradiction in Architecture," *Zodiac 17*, 1967, pp. 123-126.

"Three Projects: Architecture and Landscape, Architecture and Sculpture, Architecture and City Planning," *Perspecta 11*, 1967, pp. 103-106.

"Trois bâtiments pour une ville de l'Ohio," *L'Architecture d'aujourd'hui*, December 1967-January 1968, pp. 37-39.

1968
"A Bill-Ding Board Involving Movies, Relics and Space," *Architectural Forum*, April 1968, pp. 74-76. (Football Hall of Fame Competition.)

"On Architecture," *L'Architecture d'aujourd'hui*, September 1968, pp. 36-39.

1975
"Architecture as Shelter with Decoration on It, and a Plea for a Symbolism of the Ordinary in Architecture," 1975. (Unpublished.)

1976
"Plain and Fancy Architecture by Cass Gilbert at Oberlin," *Apollo*, February 1976, pp. 6-9.

C. WRITINGS BY DENISE SCOTT BROWN

1962
"Form, Design and the City," *Journal of the American Institute of Planners*, November 1962. (Film review.)

1963
"City Planning and What It Means to Me to Be a City Planner," March 1963. Unpublished.

"Report on the Neighborhood Garden Association," Philadelphia, March 1963. Unpublished.

1964

"Natal Plans," *Journal of the American Institute of Planners*, May 1964, pp. 161-166. (On planning in South Africa.)

1965

"The Meaningful City," *Journal of the American Institute of Architects*, January 1965, pp. 27-32. (Reprinted in *Connection*, Spring 1967.)

1966

"Development Proposal for Dodge House Park," *Arts and Architecture*, April 1966, p. 16.

"Will Salvation Spoil the Dodge House?" *Architectural Forum*, October 1966, pp. 68-71.

1967

"The Function of a Table," *Architectural Design*, April 1967.

"Housing 1863," *Journal of the American Institute of Planners*, May 1967.

"The People's Architects," *Landscape*, Spring 1967, p. 38. (Review of *The People's Architects*, ed. H. S. Ransome.)

"Planning the Expo," *Journal of the American Institute of Planners*, July 1967, pp. 268-272.

"Planning the Powder Room," *Journal of the American Institute of Architects*, April 1967, pp. 81-83.

"Teaching Architectural History," *Arts and Architecture*, May 1967.

"Team 10, Perspecta 10, and the Present State of Architectural Theory," *Journal of the American Institute of Planners*, January 1967, pp. 42-50.

1968

"The Bicentennial's Fantasy Stage," *The Philadelphia Evening Bulletin*, March 8, 1968.

"Little Magazines in Architecture and Urbanism," *Journal of The American Institute of Planners*, July 1968, pp. 223-233.

"Mapping the City: Symbols and Systems," *Landscape*, Spring 1968, pp. 22-25. (Review of Passoneau and Wurman, *Urban Atlas*.)

"Taming Megalopolis," *Architectural Design*, November 1968, p. 512. (Review of *Taming Megalopolis*, ed. H. Wentworth Eldridge.)

"Urban Structuring," *Architectural Design*, January 1968, p. 7. (Review of *Urban Structuring: Studies of Alison and Peter Smithson.*)

"Urbino," *Journal of the American Institute of Planners*, September 1968, pp. 344-46. (Review of Giancarlo de Carlo, *Urbino.*)

1969

"On Pop Art, Permissiveness and Planning," *Journal of the American Institute of Planners*, May 1969, pp. 184-186.

1970

"Education in the 1970's—Teaching for an Altered Reality," *Architectural Record*, October 1970.

"On Analysis and Design," unpublished, 1970.

"Reply to Sibyl Moholy-Nagy and Ulrich Franzen," unpublished, September 4, 1970, p. 6. (Co-op City controversy.)

1971

"Learning from Pop," and "Reply to Frampton," *Casabella*, 389/360, May-June 1971, pp. 14-46. (Reprinted in *Journal of Popular Culture*, Fall 1973, pp. 387-401.)

1974

"Evaluation of the Humanities Building at Purchase" (with Elizabeth and Steven Izenour), *Architectural Record*, October 1974, p. 122.

"Giovanni Maria Cosco, 1926-1973," *Rassegna dell' Istituto di Architettura e Urbanistica*, University of Rome, August-December 1974, pp. 127-129.

1975

"On Formal Analysis as Design Research, With Some Notes on Studio Pedagogy," unpublished, 1975.

"Sexism and the Star System in Architecture," unpublished, 1975.

"Symbols, Signs and Aesthetics: Architectural Taste in a Pluralist Society," unpublished, 1975.

1976

"House Language" (with Elizabeth Izenour, Missy Maxwell, and Janet Schueren), *American Home*, August 1976. (On "Signs of Life.")

"On Architectural Formalism and Social Concern: A Discourse for Social Planners and Radical Chic Architects," *Oppositions 5*, Summer 1976, pp. 99-112.

"Signs of Life: Symbols in the American City" (with Elizabeth Izenour, Steven Izenour, Missy Maxwell, Janet Schueren, and Robert Venturi). Text for a Bicentennial exhibition, Renwick Gallery, National Collection of Fine Arts, Smithsonian Institution, Washington, D.C., 1976.

Signs of Life: Symbols in the American City (with Steven Izenour). New York: Aperture Inc., 1976. (Exhibition catalog.)

"Suburban Space, Scale and Symbol" (with Elizabeth Izenour, Missy Maxwell, and Janet Schueren), *Via*, University of Pennsylvania, 1976. (Excerpts from "Signs of Life.")

"The Symbolic Architecture of the American Suburb," in catalog for *Suburban Alternatives: 11 American Projects*, the American Architectural Exhibition for the 1976 Venice Biennale. (Excerpts from "Signs of Life.")

"Zeichen des Lebens, Signes de Vie," *Archithese 19*, 1976.

D. WRITINGS BY ROBERT VENTURI AND DENISE SCOTT BROWN

1968
"A Significance for A&P Parking Lots, or Learning from Las Vegas," *Architectural Forum*, March 1968, pp. 37-43ff. Reprinted in *Lotus*, 1968, pp. 70-91. German translation, *Werk*, April 1969, pp. 256-266.

1969
"Learning from Lutyens," *Journal of the Royal Institute of British Architects*, August 1969, pp. 353-354. (Rejoinder to the Smithsons' interpretation of Sir Edwin Lutyens.)

"Mass Communications on the People Freeway, or, Piranesi is Too Easy," *Perspecta 12*, 1969, pp. 49-56. (In conjunction with Bruce Adams; third year studio project at Yale.)

1970
"Reply to Pawley—'Leading from the Rear'," *Architectural Design*, July 1970, pp. 4, 370. (Reply to "Leading from the Rear," *Architectural Design*, January 1970.)

1971
"Some Houses of Ill-Repute: A Discourse with Apologia on Recent Houses of Venturi and Rauch," *Perspecta 13/14*, 1971, pp. 259-267.

"Ugly and Ordinary Architecture, or the Decorated Shed," Part I, *Architectural Forum*, November 1971, pp. 64-67; Part II, December 1971, pp. 48-53. (Discussion, January 1972, p. 12.)

"Yale Mathematics Building," unpublished, 1971.

1972
Learning from Las Vegas (with Steven Izenour). Cambridge, Mass.: MIT Press, 1972.

1973
"Bicentenaire de L'Indépendence Américaine," *L'architecture d'aujourd'hui*, November 1973, pp. 63-69.

1974
"Functionalism, Yes, But . . ." in *Architecture and Urbanism*, November 1974, pp. 33-34, and in *Architecturas Bis*, January 1975, pp. 1-2.

1977
Learning from Las Vegas: The Forgotten Symbolism of Architectural Form, revised edition (with Steven Izenour). Cambridge, Mass.: MIT Press, 1977.

E. WRITINGS BY DENISE SCOTT BROWN AND ROBERT VENTURI

1968
"On Ducks and Decoration," *Architecture Canada*, October 1968, p. 48.

1969
"The Bicentennial Commemoration 1976." *Architectural Forum*, October 1969, pp. 66-69.

"Venturi v. Gowan," *Architectural Design*, January 1969, pp. 31-36.

1970
"Co-op City: Learning to Like It," *Progressive Architecture*, February 1970, pp. 64-73.

"The Highway," Philadelphia, Institute of Contemporary Art, 1970. (Text to the catalog for the exhibit by the Institute of Contemporary Art, in collaboration with Rice University and the Akron Art Institute.)

1971
Aprendiendo de Todas Las Cosas. Barcelona: Tusquets Editor, 1971. (Compilation of articles; reviews are listed under 1972 in Section A.)

F. WRITINGS BY OTHERS AT VENTURI AND RAUCH

Carroll, Virginia, Denise Scott Brown, and Robert Venturi, "Levittown et Après," *L'architecture d'aujourd'hui*, no. 163, August-September 1972, pp. 38-42.

Carroll, Virginia, Denise Scott Brown, and Robert Venturi, "Styling, or 'These houses are exactly the same. They just look different.' " *Lotus* 9, 1975. (In Italian and English; extract from *Learning from Levittown*, a study in progress.)

Hirshorn, Paul, and Steven Izenour, "Learning from Hamburgers: The Architecture of White Towers," *Architecture Plus*, June 1973, pp. 46-55.

Izenour, Steven, "Education in the 1970's—Teaching for an Altered Reality," *Architectural Record*, October 1970.

———, "Civic Center Competition for Thousand Oaks, California; Entry by Venturi and Rauch in Association with Steven Izenour and Tony Pett," *Architectural Design*, February 1971, pp. 113-114.

CREDITS

In Part I, photographs not credited were taken by faculty and students of the Learning from Las Vegas studio, Yale University.

1. Denise Scott Brown

2. Douglas Southworth

7. Allan D'Arcangelo

8. Glen Hodges

12. Glen Hodges

13. United Aerial Survey

14. Reproduced by permission of Holt, Rinehart and Winston, Publishers, from Peter Blake, *God's Own Junkyard*. Copyright 1964 by Peter Blake.

15. Robert Venturi

16. Glen Hodges

17. Giovanni Battista Nolli, *Nuova Pianta di Roma Data in Luce da Giambattista Nolli, L'Anno MDCCXLVIII*, Rome, 1748. Plate 19.

18. Landis Aerial Surveys

19, 20. Douglas Southworth

21, 22. Ralph Carlson, Tony Farmer

24-27. Ralph Carlson, Tony Farmer

23. Douglas Southworth

28. Ron Filson, Martha Wagner

29. Ralph Carlson, Tony Farmer

30, 33. Douglas Southworth

36. Las Vegas News Bureau

37-39. Photos from personal file of John F. Cahlan, Las Vegas, Nevada

40. Las Vegas News Bureau

41. Robert Venturi

42, 43. Peter Hoyt

44. Las Vegas News Bureau

47-49. Peter Hoyt

51. Caesars Palace, Las Vegas

53. Robert Venturi

55, 56. Caesars Palace, Las Vegas

57. Deborah Marum

60. Piranesi, Ron Filson, Martha Wagner

68. Ron Filson, Martha Wagner

69. Robert Venturi

70. Victor Vasarely, Galérie Denise René, Paris

71. Las Vegas Chamber of Commerce

72. Glen Hodges

73. Reproduced by permission of Holt, Rinehart and Winston, Publishers, from Peter Blake's, *God's Own Junkyard*. Copyright 1964 by Peter Blake.

74. Standard Oil Co., New Jersey

75, 76. Robert Venturi

77. Reproduced by permission of Verlag Gerd Hatje GMBH, Stuttgart, from Schwab, *The Architecture of Paul Rudolph*, Robert Perron

78. William Watkins

79. Reproduced by permission of *Progressive Architecture*, May 1967

80. The office of Venturi and Rauch

81. Robert Perron

82-86. William Watkins

87. Robert Venturi

88. Jean Roubier, Paris

90, 91. Learning from Las Vegas studio, Yale University

92. Museo Vaticano, Rome

93, 94. Robert Venturi

95. Chicago Architectural Photographing Company

96. Camera Center, Charlottesville, Virginia, or Dexter Press, Inc., West Nyack, N.Y.

99. Spencer Parsons

100. Reproduced by permission of the Museum of Modern Art, New York; Mies van der Rohe, House with Three Courts, project 1934

102, 103. Charles Brickbauer

104-106. Learning from Las Vegas studio, Yale University

107-108. Learning from Levittown studio, Yale University

110. Learning from Las Vegas studio, Yale University

111. Denise Scott Brown

112. Bryan and Shear, Ltd

113. Denise Scott Brown

114. Moshe Safdie

115, 116. David Hirsch

117. William Watkins

118. Robert Venturi

119, 120. Reproduced by permission of Architectural Book Publishing Co., from George Nelson, *Industrial Architecture of Albert Kahn*

121. Reproduced by permission of Harvard University Press, Cambridge, from Sigfried Giedion, *Space, Time and Architecture* Moholy-Dessau

122. Reproduced by permission of Architectural Press Ltd., London, from Le Corbusier, *Towards a New Architecture*

124. Reproduced by permission of Architectural Press Ltd., London, from J. M. Richards, *The Functional Tradition in Early Industrial Buildings*, Eric de Mare

125. Peter Kidson, Peter Murray, and Paul Thompson, *A History of English Architecture*, Penguin Books

126. Reproduced by permission of Harvard University Press, Cambridge, from Sigfried Giedion, *Space, Time and Architecture*

127. Reproduced by permission of Van Nostrand Reinhold Co., copyright 1967, from Peter Cook, *Architecture: Action and Plan*, Tchernikov's *101 Fantasies*

128. Reproduced by permission of Doubleday and Co., Inc.,

from R. Buckminster Fuller,
Robert W. Marks, *The Dymaxion World of Buckminster Fuller*,
copyright 1960 by R. Buckminster Fuller

130, 131. Reproduced by permission of Van Nostrand Reinhold Co., from G.E. Kidder-Smith, *Italy Builds*

132. Reproduced by permission of Verlag Gerd Hatje GMBH, Stuttgart, from Le Corbusier, *Creation is a Patient Search*

133. Henry-Russell Hitchcock, Jr.

134. Damora

136. George Cserna

137. Hellmuth, Obata and Kassabaum

138. Peter Papademetriou

139. Robert Venturi

140. Denise Scott Brown

141. Reproduced by permission of Van Nostrand Reinhold Co., copyright 1967, from Peter Cook, *Architecture: Action and Plan*

142. Learning from Levittown studio, Yale University, Robert Miller

143. Learning from Levittown studio, Yale University, Evan Lanman

144. Learning from Levittown studio, Yale University

145. Las Vegas News Bureau

146. Robert Venturi